A Generations of Heroes

Personal Accounts from the Battle of the Bulge

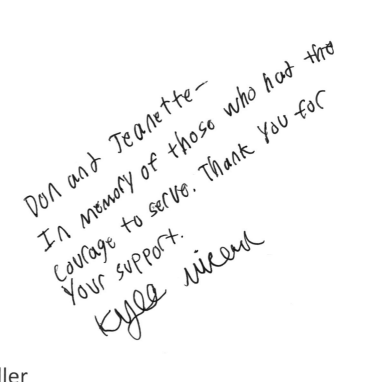

Don and Jeanette—
In memory of those who had the
courage to serve. Thank you for
your support.
Kyle Miller

Kyle Miller

A Generation of Heroes
by Kyle Miller

Published by Voices from the Front
Pickerington, Ohio 43147

Voices from the Front is a non-profit organization seeking to preserve the
stories of our nation's veterans. To learn more about Voices from the
Front, Kyle Miller, and the mission visit our website at
www.voicesfromthefront.org

ISBN: 978-0-557-96543-4

"Freedom is not free, but the [U.S. military] will pay most of your share."

-Ned Dolan
Captain, USMC

Table of Contents

Why bother?   6
The Greatest of Battles   8
The Beginning of the End   9

FRANK WALSH   15

RICHARD WHEELER   19

Out of the Woods   22

MILES MCFARLAND   33

ALBERT LESHY   35

ROBERT MOLLENAUER   44

We Shall Never Surrender   46

OKEY E. TAYLOR   52

PAUL KROUSE   57

WILLIAM (BILL) RUTH   63

The Attack of the Rising Sun   71

PAUL (GENE) KOHLI   79

RICHARD LEE LYNAM   87

LAWRENCE BOTT   88

The "Soft Underbelly" of Europe   95

ALTON LITSINBERGER   105

DANTE TONEGUZZO   111

The Great Crusade   119

Don Dill   137

Wendell Ellenwood   141

   In the Heat of Winter   **144**

Eddie Leibbrand   152

Rupert "Twink" Starr   156

   Victory in Europe   **163**
   Notes and References   **167**
   Voices from the Front   **169**

Why bother?

IF YOU ARE READING THIS, my assumption is you have seen the cover, and you know this book is about the individual stories of veterans of World War II, specifically the Battle of the Bulge. The goal of this book is to preserve these veterans' stories so they will outlive the veterans themselves. But you may ask yourself, why bother? Why is preserving a few men's personal experiences so important? Do we really need another book on World War II? We are never going to forget it.

That is true; we will never forget World War II. How could we forget a war that claimed over 50 million lives and left many more devastated? How could we forget a war with such brutal fighting that stretched from the African desert to the frigid Scandinavian mountains, from the crowded streets of London to the tropical island of Guadalcanal? How could we forget a war that violated human rights on a scale never seen before or since in the concentration camps of Germany? The truth is, we will never forget the war, its scale, its devastation, its battles, and the political and military leaders that led their nations to victory or defeat.

There are enough books documenting these facts of the war to fill a warehouse. But perhaps the most important part of the history of World War II has been under-recorded for decades, and large parts of it have been lost. This part of history is the individual experiences of those who lived and fought in this greatest of wars. Those whose lives were in constant danger, who saw events of the war unfold in front of them, in real time, with no idea on what the outcome would be. These men offer a unique perspective to the war that not even the most detailed book, map, or photograph can offer. These soldiers lived and influenced one of the most critical times in human history. Their stories are the best way for people today to understand and feel the emotions, thoughts, and attitudes of those involved in World War II. The veterans of World War II provide a bridge to the past, one that is far easier to relate to personally than any book or movie on the war. Sadly, this connection is quickly disappearing -- one thousand World War II veterans die every day. Every day, one thousand of the people who experienced the largest war in history firsthand leave this Earth forever, and responsibility is passed on to the living to remember their stories and preserve them for the next generation. Five of the veterans who shared their stories with me died before the publication of this book.

One of the First World War II veterans I met was a former Paratrooper named Richard Wheeler. Our first meeting opened my eyes to a sad reality -- my generation is the last to see a living World War II veteran. The next will not have the living connection to World War II that we have today. It is up to those of us, living in the present, to preserve the stories of those who lived and fought in the Second World War, so that who they are and what they did will be remembered by all future generations, even after the men themselves have left this world.

The Greatest of Battles

THIS BOOK DETAILS THE PERSONAL experiences of the Litsinberger Chapter of Veterans of the Battle of the Bulge. They are the victors and survivors of the largest battle the United States has ever fought. They are among the tens of thousands of young soldiers whose strength and heroism in the Ardennes forest during the bitter cold winter of 1944-45 brought about the destruction of Hitler's Reich and the beginning of the world we know today. It is because of their bravery, honor, and sacrifice that our country has thrived, and our freedom has survived.

The Beginning of the End

THE SECOND WORLD WAR WAS the largest, most devastating war in human history. Millions of young men had been killed and injured in battle, countless homes and families destroyed, entire cities lay in rubble, vast fields and forests ravaged. In concentration camps across Europe, millions of women and children were being executed in lethal gas chambers; men were being worked to death, all because of their ethnicity and religion. In almost every family from the Soviet Union to the United States, at least one member was absent, off fighting a war, with the terrifying idea of never reuniting with their families hanging over their heads.

In the months before the Battle of the Bulge, this devastation, genocide, and fear had haunted the world for nearly five years, and showed no sign of coming to a close. As long as one man, Adolf Hitler, and his fanatical supporters known as the Nazi party, remained in power in Germany, this most terrible of wars would drag on.

A failed Austrian-born artist and World War I veteran, Adolf Hitler had seized power in Germany by manipulating those struggling in the Great Depression and humiliated by the nations elimination, and elimination of anyone who got in his way. Though his first attempt to overthrow the government resulted in his arrest and conviction of high treason, he was released just nine months after his conviction, and his popularity continued to rise. In 1933, he became Chancellor of Germany, and the following year, President Paul von Hindenburg died. Hitler used this vacancy to seize power and declared himself Führer of the German Reich.

After World War I, the victorious Allies imposed heavy restrictions on the German military in the Treaty of Versailles, limiting the army's size to no more than 100,000 troops; ships were to be no larger than 10,000 tons; and the creation of an air force or tanks was forbidden. In addition to this, the Treaty also demanded Germany accept blame for starting the war and the payment of war reparations to France and England. Hitler violated all the restrictions imposed by the Treaty of Versailles and refused to continue the payment of war reparations. Despite all of this, the newly formed League of Nations (an early version of the United Nations) did little more than condemn Germany's violations, which didn't bother Hitler at all. In early 1938 he annexed Austria and part of Czechoslovakia. Both times, the League caved to Hitler's demands in the name of appeasement. They argued that if they gave Hitler some of what he wanted, he would be content and would become less aggressive. After he seized the Sudetenland, a region that made up about 20% of Czechoslovakia, Hitler promised he would lay claim to more of his neighbors' territory, and British Prime Minister Neville Chamberlain proclaimed that Europe had secured "peace for out time." He could not have been more wrong.

The early-morning silence shattered across the Polish border as the sounds of roaring plane engines passed overhead, the grinding of tank tracks drew closer, and the pounding of marching soldiers followed close behind. It was the morning of September 1, 1939 and from that morning on, the world would never be the same. The night before, the Nazis had caused almost two dozen "incidents," mainly the burning of buildings, anti-German radio broadcasts, and the killing of Gestapo prisoners dressed as Polish soldiers. These staged "incidents" along the German-Polish border were intended to portray Poland as taking aggressive actions against innocent Germans, thereby giving Hitler the rationalè to launch his preplanned invasion.

The most destructive war in human history began as the German air force, the Luftwaffe, attacked Polish towns and airfields along the border. Contrary to popular belief, the Polish air force was not destroyed in this opening phase of battle. The Luftwaffe chose to focus mainly on major towns, along with military communication and logistic lines. But the small and underequipped Polish air force was outdone by its German counterpart and within in a few days was rendered an irrelevant force, giving the Germans total air superiority. Within two weeks the Polish army had been broken into fragmented, disorganized units. Then, on September 17, any hope the Poles still had of holding out vanished literally overnight as more than 800,000 Soviet troops invaded the country from the east. The surprise Soviet intervention came from a non-aggression pact the Soviet Union and Nazi Germany had made less than a month earlier. The agreement shocked everyone because of Hitler's well-known hatred of communism. The treaty officially recognized each nation's government and established German and Soviet "spheres of influence." But there was another clause that was not made public. A clause that split Poland between the two power hungry nations, and which sealed Poland's doom before the war had begun.

The government ordered the evacuation of as many military units as possible to England and France and then left the country to form a government in exile.

Units that could not be evacuated either surrendered or fought until the bitter end. On September

29, Warsaw fell after a brutal siege, and by October 2, all remaining Polish strongholds had collapsed. Just five weeks after the first German bombs had been dropped over Poland, the conflict was over. The entire world's attention now focused on Europe, stunned by the swiftness of the German victory and by the once unimaginable alliance between Nazi Germany and the Soviet Union.

With Poland now firmly under his iron fist, Hitler hoped that the issue of his unjustified conquest would become moot. Up until this time, aside from a few small skirmishes along the border with France and with the Allied Navies in the Baltic and Atlantic, there had been no real fighting between Germany and the western Allies. Since they had been willing to allow him to expand his Reich's territory in the past to avoid a fullscale conflict, Hitler sent them a peace offer, hoping they would accept his occupation of Poland and another European war could be averted. But Hitler had crossed a line from which he could not step back. Britain and France rejected his olive branch out of hand. As far as the Allies were concerned, Hitler had to go. With diplomatic options off the table, both sides prepared for the conflict they knew was inevitable. Despite the fact both sides were officially at war, the French-German border saw very little actual fighting. A period that became known as the Phony War had begun, with both sides arming themselves for battle but neither taking the initiative. This time of inaction dragged through the winter and into the spring of 1940. But while no war might have existed on the battlefield, in the planning rooms of military commanders and government officials, plans were being drawn up, debated, torn down, and rewritten. The leaders of both the Allies and the Germans worked all day and late into the nights, trying to create a solid plan to deal with the fight they knew was coming.

When the time came, it would be the Germans who made the first move.

On April 9, 1940, the Phony War ended as German troops crossed the border into Denmark, overrunning the country in barely two hours. Across the Baltic Sea, German paratroopers, the first ever deployed in combat, landed in Norway. Like the Danish, the Norwegian military was caught by total surprise, giving the advantage to the outnumbered paratroopers, who quickly captured several key ports and cities. Soon, German reinforcements arrived by ship and the Norwegians, still scattered and disorganized, were soon on the defensive. Despite the confusion, the Norwegians put up a stiff fighting retreat. A brave stand by units at Midtskogen gave the King and his government time to escape, and several German troop transports were sunk by mines and in naval combat. But despite the most courageous and determined resistance, the German soldiers benefited from better weapons, training, and complete air control. As their numbers grew, the Norwegians were simply overwhelmed and began a fullscale withdrawal to the North to wait for Allied support. The first British and French troops arrived in Norway on April 14; they soon joined forces with the remnants of the Norwegian army and began to engage the Germans. Even with more Allied troops pouring into Norway, the Allies were unable to retake the territory the Germans had occupied. The arrival of The Allies stalled the German advance and despite continuous brutal fighting, neither side had much success in gaining any ground. Unless something drastic happened that would change the course of events, Norway looked like it might

become a bloody stalemate. Then, something drastic happened.

Frank Walsh
June 1, 1923 – October 31, 2010

Francis Edward "Frank" Walsh was born in Columbus, Ohio, on June 1, 1923. Frank grew up on the west side of town with a fondness for playing sports, particularly baseball.

Frank enlisted on December 4th, 1942. His strong sense of patriotic duty lead him to enlist even after failing the Marine Corp physical in October of the same year.

As a Private First Class, Frank was assigned to 3rd Platoon Regiment Company 70, 5th TDBm as a rifleman. Frank was in Heerlean, Holland, when the Battle of the Bulge began.

On December 16, 1944, during WWII, 250,000 German troops with 1000 tanks attacked through the Ardennes Woods. Facing them were just 80,000 American soldiers with 400 tanks. Frank Walsh was a private first class in a tank destroyer brigade near the German city of Achaean in December.

On the 18th of December, two days into the battle, Frank's platoon received orders to head to Bastogne, Belgium, where the Germans were closing in on the town. After arriving in Bastogne that evening, Frank's twenty-three man platoon was sent out to make contact with the Germans. As they drove down the road in the pitch dark and freezing cold, suddenly somebody in the platoon yelled "stop!" The order came just in time. A group of American soldiers from the 101st Airborne were on both sides of the road. Thinking in the dark that Frank's convoy was German and were about to ambush them they yelled "stop" in English. This made them hold their fire in time. After this near friendlyfire incident, Frank's platoon decided to return to the assembly area for the night.

The next day, December 19, Frank's platoon was sent out again to try to make contact with the Germans. When they made it a good distance down the road, they parked their vehicles and were waiting for orders to dig in, when American paratroopers came running by them and back to Bastogne. Frank's platoon then joined them in the fall back to the city. Again at the assembly area, they received new orders, to secure a nearby village and set up an outpost there. After arriving they found at least 100 Germans moving around in the trees outside the village. The Americans called for artillery strikes in the woods. The strikes never came. That night, temperatures dipped to below freezing and all of the platoon's weapons froze. If the Germans attacked that night, they would have been doomed, as they were outnumbered and had no way to fire back. Fortunately, the attack never came. The next day, the platoon went back to Bastogne to talk to their company's commander. They told him they needed more soldiers, given the fact Germans around the village outnumbered them 4:1 or more.

The commander agreed to strengthen the platoon, giving them two men (making them a much stronger and superior force!). Later that day, the now twenty-five man platoon headed back to the village. When they arrived, the Germans were firing flying bombs at Bastogne, some of which flew directly over their heads. One of the bombs fell short and wounded a man in the platoon. Frank was ordered to take the man back to base for medical attention while the rest of the platoon secured the village. After giving the man to the medics on base, Frank headed back to the village in his jeep. As he drove back to his platoon's position, a couple of mortar rounds landed mere feet from the road, spraying him with dirt, but fortunately not harming him. When he got back to the village, the platoon was gone. As Frank prepared to search for them he suddenly heard someone calling for help from the other side of the road. Not able to see whoever it was, Frank jumped from the jeep and took cover behind a dirt pile alongside the road. He didn't know if the man was an American who really needed help, or an English-speaking German, setting a trap, as they were known to do so during the Battle of the Bulge. To see if there were Germans on the other side he poked his helmet above the dirt pile. Gunfire erupted immediately and bullets slammed into Frank's helmet and cover. He knew there were Germans on the other side now. But the man was still calling for help, so he must have been an American. But Frank couldn't help him; he was alone, armed with little more than a first-aid pack and the Germans were closing in. Behind that dirt pile, alone in the frozen Ardennes forest, Frank made the hardest decision of his life. Unable to help the man still calling for help, Frank slipped away and continued to search for his platoon -- a decision he still regretted, 65 years later.

Frank eventually found his platoon in another part of the village. There, he learned the man calling for help was another injured platoon member, who was later found dead. This only compounded the intense guilt Frank already felt, and even when he shared this story six and half decades later, he still could not help but cry when he talked about being unable to save his fellow soldier.

For a few more days, the platoon remained on guard duty in the village before returning to base. There they got to take their boots off for the first time since December 18. Their feet swelled very badly, and one man discovered he had frostbite. Their mission for the next day had to be canceled; however, after a brief recovery time, they continued to operate in the area until January 1945.

After the end of World War Two, Frank remained in Europe for several months before arriving back in the states on December 1, 1945. There, he was discharged as an Officer with the rank of 2nd Lieutenant, which he had achieved through a Battlefield Commission during the war. The first thing Frank did upon returning to the United States was call his mother.

For his service, 2nd Lieutenant Frank Walsh received the Good Conduct Medal, Purple Heart, Bronze Star, Merit Citation, and the Belgian Croix de Guerrè.

Frank married a woman named Catherine on April 27, 1946. Together, they had six children; Kathleen, Mary Margaret, Jeremiah, June, Diane, and Carole. During his civilian career he worked as a railroad engineer for both steam and diesel engines. Today, the greatest thing that makes Frank smile is when you ask him about his thirteen grandchildren and seven great grandchildren.

At 85 years old, this loyal veteran of the Battle of the Bulge still remembers vividly the great number of casualties caused by the battle, but stands proud of his service to his country, his family, and to history.

This is the story of one man who, like millions of others, put their own lives on the line, to protect our freedom and to restore freedom to those who lost it.

Richard Wheeler
April 18, 1924 – June 17, 2011

Richard Hugh Wheeler was born on April 18, 1924 in Spaulding, Idaho although his family later moved to Tacoma, Washington. As a young boy he loved to go to his Uncle Ed's farm and see all the animals. His favorite animal was a sway back horse that always followed him around the farm. He loved it so much that when he was five he asked his Uncle if he could keep it. Sarcastically, Uncle Ed told him he could keep the horse if it fit in the car. Like all five year-olds would, Richard thought his Uncle was serious; he tried to convince his Dad to put the horse in the car. His Dad tried to explain that the horse would not fit. But Richard didn't believe him and was driven to tears when his dad wouldn't even try. To this day Richard still thinks the horse would have fit if his dad had tried.

Drafted into the military on his high school graduation day, June 5, 1943, Richard had days to pack and says his good-byes were short and sweet. Traveling by train across the United States, he arrived at Camp Taccoa, Georgia on June 25, at the tender age of 19. Training to become a paratrooper proved very difficult. The instructors were tough and recruits began to feel hated and many wanted to quit. Temperatures usually ranged between 95 and 105 degrees as the recruits did continuous, vicious exercises in the extreme heat. All were pushed to their physical limit and some beyond. Richard passed out during exercises on day and spent four days in the hospital. Determined to become a paratrooper he refused to quit and his hard work was eventually rewarded when he completed his training, and became part of the

517th Parachute Infantry Combat Team as an artillery man.

The 517th deployed to Italy. Then on August 15, 1944 the unit landed in southern France, Richard took point for a group of soldiers as they advanced, Being ahead of the group Richard was the first to encounter a German machine gun nest. Attempting to put suppressing fire on the Germans he emptied an entire clip of 30. caliber bullets into the machine gunner's position. A fellow soldier quickly came to Richard's aid and set up his powerful 50. caliber machine gun. Richard quickly moved behind the man to avoid being deafened by the gun's roar, as it eliminated the German position.

When the Battle of the Bulge began, Richard was on the front line in southern France. But he soon found himself being sent north to combat the Germans in the Ardennes. He arrived to find the Germans were not the only enemy they faced. The Belgian winter proved to be harsh. Temperatures would get as low as -10, often the Americans were not equipped for such conditions and struggled stay warm. The men firing the Howitzer artillery pieces moved almost every other day to support new orders as the battle raged, rarely stopping, hardly sleeping, and always freezing. Every time his unit stopped, Richard had to dig a foxhole; just deep enough to crouch in, and remain there until ordered to do otherwise. The men's endurance, already stretched, nearly cracked when one man came down with scabies. Everyone in the unit was forced to strip from their uniforms and shower in the winter snow. Despite all the enemy engagements he had seen, this was the one time Richard truly believed he was going to die. The men's dirty uniforms were washed as well, but not dried, and with only one pair, they had no choice but to put on the soaking uniforms. The only way to dry them was to sleep in them through the night. The memory of the bitter weather has never faded from Richard's mind or body. In the aftermath of the battle of the bulge he suffered from frost bitten feet, damaging the nerves in his feet so to this day he can't tell whether his feet are hot or cold. After the liberation of St. Vith, Richard remained there for the rest of the battle.

Private First Class Richard Wheeler returned to America in August 1945 to embrace his mother and father; he married Florence F. Harris and together they had three children Hugh, Susan, and Martin. After the war Richard worked to support his family in both farming and civil service. Sadly Florence died of heart problems in July 1996. Shortly before her death Florence asked "Has Richard found a wife yet?" knowing he would need one. After his Florence's death Richard met Katharine Kramer a former English teacher, they married on October 3, 1999 and have been happily married since.

What makes Richard most proud of his service is the pride to be a paratrooper. He is proud to have made it through one of the toughest training programs in the military. Nothing makes him sad about his service and he is grateful to have had no nightmares of what he saw in the war and does not dwell on what he has seen or done. When asked what wants everyone to remember most about World War II, and all wars for that matter, it is that the true heroes are in cemeteries.

Out of the Woods

WHILE THE TWO WARRING SIDES continued the brutal clash in Norway, a more important battle was about to begin over 700 miles to the south. All along western Germany, the German army set into motion what would be one of the most important and, indeed, one of the most historic campaigns of the Second World War. As the sky grew dark, units took up their positions along the border and waited for morning. As soon as the sun rose on May 10, 1940, one of the most decisive battles in history began. In the Netherlands and Belgium, people who had gone to sleep in countries that had declared neutrality awoke to the sound of plane engines as the German Luftwaffe began to bomb military installations and drop paratroopers over key bridges to secure them for the main army. Along the borders, German tanks followed by infantry began the attack on Dutch and Belgian positions. In the Netherlands, the Dutch, while surprised, reacted quickly, isolating or capturing enemy paratroopers dropped deep into the country. But in the face of the main German invasion force, the Dutch withdrew inland, blowing bridges to slow the enemy advance. To the south, French army units, joined by the British Expeditionary Force, or BEF, began their preplanned reaction by advancing into Belgium.

In preparing a defensive plan, the Allies envisioned the Germans would repeat their opening offensive in World War I, sending the main thrust of the attack through Belgium to outflank the virtually impregnable defenses of the French Maginot line, which ran along the whole border with Germany. Not wanting to get caught off guard as they had been in 1914, the Allies stationed some of their best units in Northern France, ready to march into Belgium the moment the Germans attacked. The Belgians just had to hold the Germans at the border long enough for the Allies to get entrenched, and time was on their side. Or so they thought.

As the first German units entered Belgium, they faced strong resistance from Belgian forces in well-entrenched positions, the most ominous of which was Fort Eben-Emael, the most modern fortress in the world, and believed impenetrable. As long as the Belgians held it, they would have control over the main roads leading into their country, making a German advance nearly impossible. To remove this obstacle, the Germans devised a bold and unprecedented plan to neutralize the fort, using gliders to land paratroopers on the roof of the fortress and using hollow charges to enter from above. This unique insertion began with the initial stage of the campaign. Gliders carrying German assault teams landed on the roof, taking the fort garrison completely off guard. Unprepared and disorganized, the Belgians at Eben-Emael soon surrendered, and German troops took control of the nearby bridges the Fortress was meant to defend. Soon German troops were pouring into the country, and the shocked Belgians began to retreat to other positions deeper in the interior.

With the German Army storming into Belgium and the Netherlands, the Allies now raced to get into entrenched positions east of Brussels. From their point of view, the fate of the entire battle hinged on whether the Allies could get firmly dug in and prepared before the Germans arrived. What the Allies didn't know was that the attack on Belgium was just a diversion; the heart of the German invasion plan focused on a small section of the frontline, on the French and Belgian border, a densely wooded area called the Ardennes.

As brutal and chaotic fighting raged in the North, the bulk of the German army moved through the quiet Ardennes woods. Centered on the border between France, Belgium, and Luxembourg, the Ardennes was a large forest, with small villages and only a few dirt roads. The relatively rural area would not be seen as a priority to any military. It was believed impossible to get an army of any substantial size through the forest, along those narrow and twisted dirt roads, surrounded by dense clusters of trees. Traffic jams would be inevitable, slowing any army's advance and making the troops vulnerable to attack from the air. With these difficulties surrounding the Ardennes, no one could predict that this quiet, peaceful forest would be at the heart of two of the most decisive battles in human history. The second would not occur for another four-and-half year, but the first began on that warm May day as German tanks and soldiers pushed through the believed impenetrable woods.

They encountered little resistance as they pushed through the forest. The Allies had virtually no troops stationed in the area, believing the Germans would not actually attempt the impossible task of forcing a huge army along those narrow and twisted dirt roads, surrounded by dense clusters of trees and so vulnerable to attack from the air. The idea was so unrealistic that even as the first units were spotted moving through the woods on the morning of May 10th, the French and British believed the units to be a distraction and that the simultaneous attack in Belgium was the real German offensive.

But as they day wore on, the French and Belgian units became increasingly surprised by the sheer number of Germans they encountered. Soon they were forced to fall back to the Meuse River, where they established strong defensive positions along the west bank. The German troops were slow to pursue as the undeveloped roadways began to work against them and massive traffic jams ensued, a perfect target for Allied bombers. But no bombers came. The Allied high generals were painfully aware that their air force was no match for the Luftwaffe so close to Germany and did not want to risk losing its sparse bombers. Besides, the French were digging in along the Meuse, and it would be weeks before the Germans would be prepared to launch a full scale attack across the river.

But the invaders had no intention of launching a conventional assault, knowing it would take too long to organize for a plan that depended solely on speed. On May 12, the Germans launched several companies across the Meuse near the city of Seden, into the teeth of a much larger French force. To compensate for the small number of troops on the ground, the Luftwaffe organized its biggest bombing of the war. Hundreds of German planes bombarded French positions throughout the day. The air strikes broke the will of the French, and soon a small force of German soldiers had established a foothold on the west bank of the Meuse. The shock of the surprise attack sent chaos through the French ranks. Rumors spread, and it became impossible to decipher what was true. A gap soon formed in the French lines when a regiment panicked and retreated when hearing that German troops had gotten behind them. In fact, not a single German tank had crossed the river yet.

Exploiting the enemy's confusion, German engineers finished constructing three bridges across the river. German tanks and infantry reinforcements began pouring over the river, and the French completely collapsed. Realizing now that the attack through the Ardennes was no longer a diversionary skirmish, but a major offensive, the Allies ordered every available bomber to destroy the bridges and cut off the flow of German troops across the Meuse. The bombers made their attack but the Luftwaffe intervened and prevented the Allies from destroying any of their targets and causing them heavy casualties. With the failure to eliminate the bridges went any chance the Allies had of preventing a German breakout into mainland France. On May 15, five days after the initial German attack, the Panzer (tank) units under General Erwin Rommel broke out of the Meuse bridgehead and began the German Race to the Sea.

The same day, as Rommel's tanks smashed through French units in their march to the west, the Netherlands surrendered to the Germans. Caught between the Dutch collapse in the North and the German threat on their own territory, the Allied command was thrown into disarray. Most French troops were either stationed at the Maginot line on the border with Germany or had been deployed to Belgium to stop the German attack there. This meant there were few French units, most importantly tanks, close enough to immediately launch a counterattack against the Germans. This lack of organization proved to be fatal, as isolated French units surrendered or were destroyed by the quick and devastating German Panzer attacks. With Rommel leading the charge, the German tanks advanced thirty miles in just 24 hours, an achievement so great it even surprised the Germans.

While the Allies seemed to be staring defeat in the face, the Germans felt almost exactly the same way. Many in the German high command, including Hitler himself, were worried they had bitten off more than they could chew. The attack through the Ardennes had thus far succeeded beyond his wildest dreams, but Hitler worried that Rommel had gone too far. The German Panzers had moved far ahead of the German infantry, and the gap between the two was dangerously wide. A French counterattack could easily cut off and destroy Rommel and his tanks, eliminating the tip of the German spear and the German chance for victory with it. The Panzers had been forced to stop to give the men time to rest and repair the tanks, giving the Allies crucial time to reorganize their forces. Hitler's fears seemed to be confirmed when French tanks led by Colonel Charles De Gaulle attacked the German 1st Panzer division as it rested and regrouped at the town of Montcornet, though the Germans managed to organize quickly enough to repulse the attack. The key to German success in breaking up the French attack was the Luftwaffe. The Allied air force had been badly crippled in the opening days of the campaign by the larger and better equipped Luftwaffe, which now enjoyed total dominance of the sky.

On May 19, Hitler decided to allow the Panzer divisions to continue their advance to the English Channel after being told by his Generals that waiting any longer would be fatal. After beating off a second counterattack by De Gaulle's forces, the Germans smashed through nearby British divisions that had returned from Belgium, and raced towards the Channel. The next day the first German tanks reached the coast. In just ten days, the German Panzers had advanced straight across northern France and split the Allied Army in two, with the combined French, British, and Belgian forces to the North and the rest of the French Army to the south.

The Allied high command, still shocked by the swiftness of the unexpected German assault, was unable to come up with a plan to reunite the separated armies in France and Belgium. The Allies did have a window of opportunity to reverse their defeats while German Panzers were thinly spread and were waiting for the infantry to catch up. But when the French Prime Minister removed his top general because of his failure to halt the German Blitzkrieg, the transition of leadership delayed all planning, and the Allies' window of opportunity was lost. Several small counterattacks were launched by the British and French forces, but these attacks were uncoordinated and poorly planned, allowing the Germans sufficient time to react and push back the attackers.

Despite the Germans' tightening noose around the Allied armies in Belgium and any opportunity of linking forces with the French to the south gone, the high command still hoped to arrange their soldiers in defensive positions along the Belgian coast. But by May 23, even hope that this plan could succeed evaporated, as German troops and aircraft threatened the ports needed to supply forces in Belgium.

Realizing their position had become untenable, the Allies began a fighting retreat. With brave soldiers holding back the German onslaught the main allied force began to move into the large Belgian ports, while across the English Channel, the British were gathering every vessel available for a desperate operation to save the men trapped against the coast, an operation code named Dynamo.

Every ship imaginable, from large troop carriers to small sailboats, any vessel that could make the trip across the English Channel, gathered in southern England. The first ships set sail on May 26. More would follow in the coming days, as hundreds of ships, whether in groups or alone, sailed from England over the days to come.

Despite the many different ships and times of arrival, all had the same destination -- a port on the Belgian coast called Dunkirk. While the ships plowed through the channel waters, in the port tens of thousands of British and French soldiers gathered. Surrounded by the German army, these soldiers held on to one hope, the hope that was sailing toward them as fast as possible. Operation Dynamo, the desperate attempt to save what was left of the French and British armies in Belgium, was underway, beginning as the first troops departed on ships for England. Many in the Allied high command feared they would not be able to rescue many of the troops with the Germans so close behind them. Little did they know their enemies had given them a desperately needed break. Two days before the beginning of Operation Dynamo, Hitler had ordered all German units to halt and hold their positions. Historians to this day wonder why Hitler ordered his soldiers to stop. Some say that his commander of ground forces, General Gerd Von Rundstedt, told him that the tanks needed to halt and be refitted, and Herman Goering, the commander of the Luftwaffe, assured the Führer that his planes could stop the evacuation. Others say his decision was politically motivated, an attempt to show the British some mercy in hopes that a peace with Great Britain could be achieved after the defeat of France. But whatever Hitler's motive, his decision essentially saved the Allies.

While the Allied air force on mainland Europe had been eliminated as a threat, the British RAF, or Royal Air Force, had kept its best planes, the Spitfires, closer to home in light of the defeat of Belgium. These reserved aircraft and their pilots were ordered to protect the evacuation from Dunkirk. With both air forces on a collision course, the result was the greatest dogfights the world had yet seen. As troops boarded ships and headed for England, in the skies above German and British pilots engaged in spectacular duels, both fighting for control of the air and ultimately the fate of Operation Dynamo. With the ease the Germans had established air superiority over their enemies in the past, it was a nasty surprise to the Luftwaffe pilots to meet an enemy whose skill and technology matched their own. In the dogfights that filled the skies for over a week, both sides lost roughly the same number of planes, and in the end the Luftwaffe failed to stop or slow the evacuation of troops from Dunkirk.

Three days after the Army halted; Hitler ordered his troops to eliminate all remaining Allied units in Belgium. But the seventy-two hour delay had given the Allies enough time to organize a rearguard defense, and the German attack became bogged down in heavy fighting, allowing the evacuation of troops to continue for days. On June 3 the evacuation finally ended as German troops reached Dunkirk. Two French divisions remained behind to protect the last troops boarding the ships and surrendered soon after the last ships departed for England.

"The Miracle of Dunkirk," as it became known, was truly a miracle of the Allies, and particularly the British. The entire British Expeditionary Force had been saved from capture, along with many French soldiers. In total, 338,226 Allied soldiers escaped the German clutches at Dunkirk, and these soldiers would play a valuable role in the battles to come.

Even though the evacuation had succeeded beyond the Allies' wildest dreams, the French in particular now faced a major problem. The soldiers saved were now in England, and had been forced to leave most of their heavy weapons in Belgium. While over 100,000 soldiers would soon be back in Europe, it would be some time before the Allies could establish a secure defensive line, and time was something the Allies did not have.

The French Army had lost its best troops and equipment in Belgium or in the Dunkirk evacuation. Army strength had been cut almost in half, and the remaining units were thinly spread and ill-equipped. But despite the precarious situation, the French morale was raised by several advantages they possessed. Since they were now fighting on home ground, they knew the terrain better than the Germans, and were also much closer to resupply depots and repair areas. The French armor units had been rebuilt and reorganized. The Germans had not accounted for these factors, so when they began their offensive into the heart of France on June 5, the resistance was far greater than expected. For the first three days, heavy fighting took place along the rivers Somme and Aisne as the Germans attempted to fight though barrages of French fire and secure bridgeheads on the other side. Their attempts were repeatedly repulsed by clever French defensive tactics. Had it not been for the dominate Luftwaffe, there is a possibility the Germans might not have broken the French lines. But the German pilots were masters of the sky, and they decimated French positions and broke up counterattacks. This proved decisive, and slowly the Germans finally established several bridgeheads, then slowly overran the French defenses. By June 9 the Germans had broke out in several areas and began to fan out across north and western France. From then on the French collapse was rapid. Rommel's Panzer division raced west towards the Brittany peninsula and had reached Cherbourg by June 18. The French government, hoping to save the nation's grand jewel, declared Paris an open city, meaning the army would not establish defenses inside the city, sparing it from the destruction of war. On June 14, 1940, German troops marched into Paris. Many French citizens watched as the soldiers, now their occupiers, arrived in hundreds, wondering what was to become of them, their city, and their country.

While the fall of Paris is to this day the symbol of the French collapse, the violence continued to the south and east, as the last French divisions continued to resist the German offensive. While some units held strong defensive positions and put up a determined fight, they were steadily overrun one by one.

On June 16, unwilling to surrender but realizing he had lost the support of his cabinet, French Prime Minister Paul Reynaud resigned. His successor, Phillippe Petain, made a public announcement that France would seek an armistice with Germany. When Hitler heard the French wanted to negotiate, he organized one of the most symbolic acts of revenge of the war.

One can hardly imagine what the French delegation felt as they boarded a railway carriage in the Compiegne Forest, the same railway carriage in which the German delegation had surrendered to the Allies in at the end of World War I. The carriage had been taken out of a museum in Paris and brought back to the same location. Hitler sat in the same chair as Allied Commander Ferdinand Foch had when he accepted the German surrender on November 11, 1918. In Hitler's twisted mind, this was the moment of supreme revenge against the French. Both sides signed the Armistice on June 22, and when it went into effect at 1:35 AM on June 25, 1940, the great superpower France had fallen.

Miles McFarland
May 16, 1923 – October 17, 2011

Miles McFarland was born in Piqua, Ohio, but spent most of his childhood in Columbus. Going to picture movies was one of his favorite activities as a child.

Drafted in January 1943, Miles did his basic training in Mississippi and was assigned to a hospital unit. He worked in the pharmacy and achieved the rank of sergeant. Miles was sent to Europe in the fall of 1944, reaching the front lines on October 13. During his seven months in Europe, Miles fought in countless battles alongside his buddies trough the hardships and losses to defeat the Nazis. Stationed in Deischoveitiz, Germany, when the Battle of the Bulge began, Miles and his comrades were sent to counter the German breakthrough. On one cold night during the battle, a lost or confused German SS officer wandered to American lines. Miles and his unit captured the officer, and Miles assigned two men to take him to company headquarters. But the two soldiers shot him on the way, claiming he had tried to escape. However, the German spoke English rather well and had been insulting the soldiers, leading Miles to believe that the men were insulted enough to kill the German. Miles came out of the Battle of the Bulge uninjured, and assisted in the attack into the German Fatherland, leading to Germany's final surrender on May 7, 1945.

Miles returned to America in February 1946. By now he held the rank of Acting Platoon Sergeant. He went to OSU College of Pharmacy, struggling to get back into the school routine. After his graduation Miles worked as a pharmacist and married in May, 1951, but never had children.

Miles is proud to have fought for his country, but saddened by the loss of some of his close friends and by the mistakes made by Allied leaders over the course of the war. He also wants everyone to remember the brutality of the Battle of the Bulge.

Albert Leshy

August 6, 1922 – August 29, 2012

The fourth child of Lebanese immigrants, Albert Leshy, or "Jake," a nickname his brother gave him that has stuck for life, was born on August 6, 1922, in St. Clairesville, Ohio. Growing up, Jake worked alongside his two older brothers and sister every day on the family farm, planting and harvesting crops. On Saturdays they would wake up at four in the morning to take their produce into town to sell at the market. Like his siblings before him, Jake worked hard in school and got good grades. His dedication to a good education paid off when Ohio State College's Tower Club accepted him, allowing him to avoid the regular tuition his family couldn't afford to pay.

Jake was in his sophomore year, planning to major in business, when the United States entered the Second World War. As he was not old enough to be drafted, Jake elected to continue his studies and particularly the Army ROTC (Reserve Officer Training Course.) He had begun his freshman year, which was mandatory in the pre-war era. Jake remained in college for another year and voluntarily stayed in the ROTC, when in November 1942, Congress lowered the draft age from 21 to 18, making him eligible. The commanding officer of the College ROTC told Jake and the other one hundred students they had two choices; volunteer to immediately become an officer in the Army, or leave ROTC and be eligible to be drafted at anytime. The entire class decided to volunteer. In early 1943, Jake Leshy left his family and Ohio State for Fort Bragg, North Carolina, to begin basic training.

Boot camp was an eye-opening experience for Mr. Leshy in more ways than one. While at Fort Bragg he got a shocking request from a number of recruits when mail call came. Could he read them their letters from home? This greatly touched Mr. Leshy; here were grown men who had come from poor backgrounds, being trained to fight a war, when they couldn't read a word of English.

After basic training, Mr. Leshy was sent to Fort Sill in Oklahoma for training to become an artillery officer. But his training soon came to a halt when he became needed elsewhere. It turned out the Army had an abundance of trained artillery officers, but had a desperate shortage of infantry officers, due to casualties. Mr. Leshy soon found himself converted to an Infantry Officer, and after additional training at Fort Benning, Georgia, Jake Leshy became a commissioned 2nd Lieutenant in the Army. After taking the massive cruiser, Queen Mary, to England, Mr. Leshy crossed the channel and landed in Normandy, France, in September of 1944. From there he was taken directly to the front, his assignment, I Company of the 1st Infantry Division. He arrived at company headquarters at 1700 hours and the Captain told him he would be commander 1st Platoon, whose commanding officer had recently been killed in action. As it was too late to introduce Mr. Leshy to the men that evening, the captain pointed to a foxhole in view in the distance and told him to spend the night there and he would meet his men in the morning. As Mr. Leshy reached the foxhole, he came upon a terrible sight, one that would forever be etched clearly in his mind. Just ten feet from his position lay a dead American soldier. Mr. Leshy didn't sleep at all that night.

The next day he met the men who were now under his commanded. Then he watched with grief as the dead from yesterday's battles were thrown like logs into the back of a truck and driven away. Shortly after his arrival at the front lines, Mr. Leshy was happy to receive a letter from his sister. Inside was a St. Christopher's medal which Mr. Leshy would carry with him for the rest of the war, and every day after that. For over two months Mr. Leshy and his men gradually fought their way their way through bitter German resistance into the western fringes of the fatherland. In December, as an award for everything the unit had accomplished, they were given two weeks of R&R (Rest and Relaxation) in southern Belgium. After establishing camp in a barn, they had portable showers set up, their first in weeks.

Five days into the company's break, they received word that they were moving out. The Germans had broken through Allied lines in the Ardennes area and the Battle of the Bulge had begun. Rushed east to reinforce the crippling American defenses, Mr. Leshy and Company I took up defensive positions at Elsenborn Ridge facing the northernmost spear of the German attack forces. For the next month, in bitter cold and over two feet of snow, the men held their ground as the Germans launched attack after attack to take the ridge. Besides the night patrols, Mr. Leshy and the others made no immediate advances against the enemy as the Germans were still too strong in the area to defeat in open battle. But by the end of January, the situation had changed; the German offensive halted and the Allies were on the offensive. Mr. Leshy participated in the Big Red One's counterattack, throwing back the weakened German forces and helping return the front line to its early December position.

With spring came a renewal of the Allied offensive, as men like Mr. Leshy broke through German lines and reached the Rhine River, the last natural barrier separating them from the German interior. The Germans had detonated all but one of the bridges leading over the river, so Mr. Leshy and his men crossed in boats near the city of Cologne. From the river banks, they drove eastward into Bavaria, Germany's southern region. They quickly seized one town after another, including the key cities of Nuremburg and Munich. It was during this time that Mr. Leshy had one of the worst experiences of his life. Though the German air force had been crippled by superior Allied airpower by this phase of the war, Mr. Leshy had a personal reminder of how dangerous a force it still was. As he and his comrades advanced across a field, they were spotted by Luftwaffe pilots, who seized the opportunity to strafe the Americans below. The plane's engines roared as they went into a dive and opened up with a barrage of machinegun fire. With no cover for protection, Mr. Leshy and the others had no choice but to throw themselves on the ground. How he escaped that attack unscathed continues to stump Mr. Leshy, but though he was not injured, he can still feel the pure terror he felt as those planes bore down on him and the others with guns blazing.

The German resistance continued on the ground as well. Firefights and artillery barrages were almost daily occurrences. By this time, Mr. Leshy had enough combat experience to detect the sound of a shell falling to earth and where it would hit. One day, as they came under fire from the Germans, Mr. Leshy heard a shell coming, and knowing it would hit close, tried to move away from the sound. But he didn't get far enough, and the explosion sent him to the ground. Another man standing nearby had his arm blown off by the shell. As Mr. Leshy lay on the ground, his captain rushed to his side. "Are you ok?" he asked."I think so" Mr. Leshy responded. "Are you sure,?"

asked the captain "'Cause you're white as a sheet." They then discovered several pieces of shrapnel had cut through Mr. Leshy's back. He was sent to a nearby hospital to have the metal removed. While most of the bigger pieces were taken out, some were burrowed too deep and since they posed no health risk, Mr. Leshy has carried them ever since.

In reflecting on these experiences, Mr. Leshy wonders to this day how he actually survived the war. How did those German planes miss him when he was trapped in an open field? How did he suffer only a few shards of shrapnel to the back, when another man roughly the same distance from the explosion lost an arm? How did he survive all the time he spent on the front lines when so many others perished? In repeatedly asking himself these questions, Mr. Leshy can reach only one conclusion; the Lord was watching out for him.

After spending a few days recovering from his injuries, Mr. Leshy returned to his unit as it continued its push toward the border with Czechoslovakia. This was the limit the division was permitted to advance. After the reaching the border they stopped and waited to link up with Soviet forces advancing from the east. By now, the war in Europe was drawing to a close. As Adolf Hitler committed suicide in his underground bunker and the Soviets overran Berlin above, German resistance effectively collapsed, and the remaining Nazi leaders surrendered unconditionally on May 7, 1945.

With the war over, Mr. Leshy's unit became part of the Occupation force. In June they were assigned to Nuremburg to guard the Nazi prisoners who were to stand trial for their war crimes. As the commanding officer, Mr. Leshy became the prison supervisor. Guarding the ex-Nazi leaders required more than preventing their escape; it also meant protecting the prisoners from themselves. Many of Hitler's subordinates had committed suicide to prevent their capture and trial, and some of those taken alive were looking for an opportunity to kill themselves before their punishment could be decided. But with a guard watching each prisoner at all times, a successful suicide attempt seemed virtually impossible. This idea was proved wrong when Herman Goring, the former commander of the German Luftwaffe and one of the top Nazi leaders to be captured, was discovered dead in his cell, mere hours before his planned execution. As the man in charge, Mr. Leshy took more heat from high command than anyone for the Nazi's suicide. Despite an intense follow-up investigation, exactly how Goring got hold of the cyanide pill he used to take his life remains a mystery. Rumors and theories have surfaced over the years, ranging from a guard giving it to him, to a secret cavity in one of Goring's teeth that contained the pill. Mr. Leshy personally believes that Goring had used his friendship with a U.S. soldier to ask for a box from his briefcase that had been taken from him after his capture. The American, unaware of what it contained, gave Goring the box. Goring then used the cyanide hidden inside to kill himself.

Though Mr. Leshy's stay at Nuremburg was hampered at times by the prisoners, his time in Europe provided the opportunities to forge some great life-long memories. In the summer of 1945 Mr. Leshy and a group of American soldiers were rewarded for their service with a vacation to Italy. During their tour of the former Axis nation, they had the opportunity to see many of the great and historical sites dating back to the time of the Roman Empire. After a visit to the capital city, the men's next destination was the Vatican. One can only imagine their combination of surprise and excitement when they were told that their group had been invited to have an audience with Pope Pius XII. They were told they could bring one object for the Pope to bless. Though he knew he wanted to bring something, Mr. Leshy had never carried any money with him during his time in Europe, since he always had his paycheck automatically sent home to support his family, so he couldn't buy anything from a local store and couldn't think of what he already had that he could have blessed by the Pope. Then he remembered the St. Christopher medal his sister had sent to him during his first days on the front lines, and that he had carried through with him every day since. What a perfect item for such a ceremony. The day he stood with his fellow soldiers, Pope Pius XII blessed each man and the objects they had brought. It remains among the greatest moments of Mr. Leshy's life. He holds on to that medal to this day.

In June 1946, after a year at Nuremburg, Lieutenant Albert Leshy finally returned home to his family. Like many young men, he used the GI bill to renew his college education. His experiences at Nuremburg sparked an interest in the court system, and Mr. Leshy decided to attend law school. After graduation he began his work as an attorney, a job he would do for fifty years. For Mr. Leshy, being an attorney wasn't just about the money; during his years practicing law, he worked for many struggling clients free of charge.

In 1954, Mr. Leshy married a woman named Constance and together they had a daughter, Pam. When his wife fell ill with cancer Mr. Leshy cared for her until her tragic passing.

On February 28, 1981, just two months after Pam's wedding, Albert Leshy married his second wife, Marilyn. During the ceremony he approached the photographer and asked "Don't we get a discount for bringing you this much business recently?" "Tell you what," the photographer replied "If you bring me back to take the pictures of your 50th anniversary I will give you a discount." Pam was taken aback by the thought "But I will be eighty by then." she protested. "Yes," said Mr. Leshy "and I will be 110."

Mr. Leshy and his second wife have been happily married for over thirty-two years. Their family has grown to include two grandchildren in this time, Joe and Rachael, both of whom have now reached adulthood.

For the shrapnel wounds he had received, Mr. Leshy was awarded the Purple Heart. In 2000, over fifty years after the war had ended, Mrs. Leshy heard about another veteran who had just received several medals he had earned during the Second World War, but never been given. Thinking her husband might be among those who had never received all the decorations they had earned for their service, she sent his discharge papers to their congresswomen, Debra Price. They discovered in their reexamination of Mr. Leshy's service that his actions in Europe had made him worthy of the Bronze Star. So it was, more than half-century after the act, the military finally awarded Albert Leshy a well-deserved Bronze Star, though he willingly admits to this day, "I don't remember what I did that earned me this medal."

Though the emotions of his war experiences are still strong, Mr. Leshy is willing to share his stories and has done several class presentations over the years. In one presentation he showed the class his Purple Heart, which has the portrait of George Washington engraved on it. One girl recognized the portrait and asked with her most serious voice "Mr. Leshy, did you know George

Washington?" " No," he responded "I'm old, but not that old."

The thing Mr. Leshy wants people to remember more than anything about the Second World War is that we got rid of Hitler. He also wants people to remember his life saying, "Old Age is not for sissies."

Robert Mollenauer

March 11, 1921 – April 29, 2000

Robert Dickson "Bob" Mollenauer was born on March 11, 1921, in Charleroi, Pennsylvania. Growing up, he spent his time hunting and playing in a nearby river. Bob also loved to build things including an intricately detailed wooden ship and a diving helmet, which he used to walk along the bottom of the river.

After graduating from high school, Bob attended the Washington and Jefferson Collage where he studied Topography (the study of Earth's features and planets, asteroids, etc). He was still in college when the Japanese attacked Pearl Harbor. He decided to continue his studies until he received his draft notice which came in late January 1943, and sadly left his family, for Fort George Meade, Maryland, on February 3.

After training, Bob joined the 333rd Infantry Regiment, part of the 84th Infantry Division in Ann Arbor, Michigan, as a mechanic. The division departed from Ann Arbor on September 24, 1944 forcing Bob to leave behind his wife Dorothy (whom he had married the previous March) and unborn child. He arrived in Scotland after a six day voyage, there training continued to until November, when the division was ordered to France. Once on mainland Europe, Bob fought alongside his buddies in western Germany pushing the farther into the enemy's homeland. When the German Ardennes offensive opened on December 16, reinforcements were ordered to halt the Axis steamroller. On December 18, the 84th division moved north to confront the German army. The weather was below zero, and German attacks were constant. Once, while on patrol alone, Bob encountered three German SS soldiers. Knowing Germany was starving at this point in the war and speaking German rather well he convinced the enemy soldiers to surrender. Despite constantly being in the heat of battle, it was eventually the winter cold that brought Bob down. The moisture in his boots combined with the fact he rarely found time to take them off resulted in trench foot. Bob was sent to a hospital in France to be treated. The doctor there wanted to amputate both feet because of the damage. But Bob insisted on attempting to heal them. Recovery was painfully slow, but steadily his feet recovered, and amputation was avoided.

Private First Class Robert Mollenauer returned home in December 1945, after more than a year in Europe. Greeting him were his parents, wife, friends and his six month old daughter, Linda who had been born while he was overseas. After his discharge Robert worked at Lee-Norse Company as a draftsman for mining machinery. This job helped him support his family which grew to include Robert Jr.

In 1951 the family moved to Columbus after Bob took a new job. There the family greeted their final child David five years later. In 1971 he took a job at Wilden Pumps, the job took them to California, where the family would settle permanently.

During his free time Bob loved to study history, especially military. He watched any war movie or reading any book he could get his hands on. Studying the bible and fishing were two other favorite pass time activities.

Bob died of Parkinson's disease on April 29, 2000 at age 79. When he died he had 5 grandchildren and had lived to see 2 Great-grandchildren.

We Shall Never Surrender

IN JUST SIX WEEKS, THE Germans had conquered all of Western Europe, faster than anyone had thought possible. With her allies gone, Great Britain now stood alone against the madman of Europe. France's swift and total collapse had surprised even the conquerors themselves. With Europe now under his control, Hitler was sure Britain would sue for peace. To his shock, the British refused to accept his peace offer, or even to negotiate. The British people, while at the moment in a very bleak hour, were determined to defeat Adolf Hitler or perish in the attempt. Prime Minister Winston Churchill proclaimed to the world, *"We shall defend our island, whatever the cost may be, we shall fight on the beaches, we shall fight on the landing grounds, we shall fight in the fields and in the streets, we shall fight in the hills, we shall never surrender."*

With England set on fighting to the bitter end, and unwilling to leave the threat the kingdom posed unaddressed, Hitler told his generals and admirals to prepare for an invasion of Britain. Codenamed operation Sea Lion, the Germans planned to land along the southeastern coast of England, establish a beachhead, and fight their way inland. The German army, with its effective fighting tactics and superior weapons, could almost certainly defeat the British army that, while large, had lost its best equipment and units in Belgium. The problem the Germans faced was not capturing Britain, but getting to it. Despite having one of the best armies in the world, the Germans lacked a strong naval fleet, and the British Royal Navy possessed the biggest and most powerful ships on the planet. Even if the German transport ships survived the Royal Navy's onslaught, which was very unlikely, the first ground troops would be heavily outnumbered and would face enemy aircraft that could attack German troops, while preventing the Luftwaffe from supporting their soldiers. The German commanders concluded that the only way operation Sea Lion stood a chance of success was if the Luftwaffe gained complete control of the air and the RAF were neutralized as a threat before the invasion began. Then the German air force could protect the transport ships from the Royal Navy and the German soldiers on the beaches during the critical moments of the initial landing.

The opening stages for this struggle for the skies that became known as the Battle of Britain began on July 10, 1940, when the Luftwaffe began to attack British shipping in the channel. The English ships were easy targets, and casualties quickly rose for the British. Because of the large number of convoys and equally large German attack groups, the RAF struggled to provide sufficient planes to escort all ships. By early August, casualties became so high that the British had no choice but to cancel all shipping through the Channel. But the real battle was yet to begin.

Codenamed Aldertag, German for "Eagle Day," was the scheduled day that the Luftwaffe would begin its main offensive against the RAF airfields and command centers. After postponement due to bad weather, Eagle Day began on August 13th. The relative peace of a faraway war the British people had grown accustomed to was shattered by the sounds of hundreds of German aircraft as they appeared in the skies over England. The Luftwaffe aircraft were met by the pilots of the RAF, and this legendary battle of the heavens began.

The German bombers targeted RAF airfields and positions, while fighters engaged in spectacular dogfights across the sky, one side trying to protect its bombers and the other trying to stop them from reaching their targets. Battles raged throughout the day as the Germans flew more and more sorties [missions] over Britain. The violence died down as night fell, but the next day the Luftwaffe returned in strength, and the dogfights and bombings resumed.

This cycle of fighting drew on for weeks as the Germans tried to cripple the RAF and the British fought simply to survive. The German pilots were surprised and shaken by the ferocity of British defense. The British Spitfire proved just as good, if not a better fighter, as the German ME 109 and Bf 110s. The British pilots benefited not just from equal skill and aircraft of that of their German counterparts, but also from a new secret weapon the Germans had not accounted for. Silent and undetectable, it allowed the British to know exactly when and where the German bombers were approaching -- a new revolution in technology called "radar".

Radio Detection and Ranging became the crux of the British defense of their island. Created by Air Marshal Hugh Dowding, the Dowding early warning system was a series of radar towers established along Britain's southern and eastern coasts. The radar sent out radio waves across the channel that bounced off objects and reported where the object was and how fast it was moving. The signals sent from the radar towers were reported back to the Strategic Fighter Command Center, where information was organized. Once the number and direction of approaching enemy aircraft were determined, the commanders then alerted the fighter pilots in the area who would fly out to meet the enemy. The system ensured the British were never caught off guard by Luftwaffe attacks, and to the Germans it became unnerving, as the RAF always seemed to be waiting for them when they reached England. The German high command were aware of the tall radar towers all along the coast and knew they must possess some importance, but because they were hard to hit and not considered relevant to the battles being fought in the sky (even though they were), the Nazis made no serious effort to destroy them.

The British benefited from fighting over their home country. The short distance planes needed to travel to meet the enemy meant the pilots could remain in the fight until their fuel was almost completely depleted. The Germans, on the other hand, had to fly across the English Channel to reach their targets and could remain in combat over England for only ten to twenty minutes before having to return to Europe. Also, although both sides could replace lost aircraft, trained and experienced pilots were harder to replace. Since combat took place over England, most British pilots who got shot down were often back in the air the same day. The German pilots, on the other hand, bailed out into a hostile country and were captured. These advantages are what gave the RAF the strength to match the previously undefeated Luftwaffe.

Despite the heavy German losses, the RAF was also taking casualties, and it was the Germans who picked the time and location of each attack. The almost unbroken waves of attacks were leaving the pilots in a constant state of exhaustion. Many men would fall asleep as soon as their planes hit the runway tarmac. Their clarity of thought became fogged and reflexes slowed, making flying even more dangerous. By early September, the RAF was on the verge of cracking as its pilots were breaking down from sheer exhaustion.

But on September 7, the Germans suddenly gave the RAF an unintentional break. Discouraged by the ferocious British resistance and heavy casualties the German commanders decided to switch the targets of the attacks to the large British cities, particularly London. The objective of the raids was to break the will of the British people to continue the fight. The terror bombings of London, which would become the most memorable part of the battle, now began, but the climax had already passed. The bombings killed many British citizens and brought horrendous destruction to the city. But the Germans had made a crucial mistake. With all bombers now targeting civilians, there was no longer any danger to the RAF airfields. This was just the break the British pilots needed, and within days, the Royal Air Force was rested and refitted to maximum strength. German casualties began to mount once again and, on September 15, the Luftwaffe lost 60 aircraft in one day's fighting. For Hitler and his commanders, any hope of launching operation Sea Lion in 1940 was lost that day.

Hitler ordered the invasion of England be postponed until the spring of 1941, but the attacks on British cities were to continue, in an attempt to lower the public's morale. The Battle of Britain would continue until the end of October. As German bombers continued to strike at innocent civilians, many British children were evacuated to the countryside. Those that remained in the cities would spend most nights in bomb shelters. Many families were separated, and many people lost their homes, possessions, and sometimes their lives. But despite all the terror that continued to fly over their island, the British had won. The Germans could not launch a land invasion for at least another six months, and the RAF, while unable to stop all the bombings, held to its superiority in the skies. The bombings of civilian targets failed in their objective as well. Even with all the horror of the Luftwaffe raids, the British resolve was never weakened, nor was there ever a voice calling to negotiate with Hitler.

The most amazing part of the entire Battle was that the fate of millions was decided by roughly 1,500 men of the Royal Air Force. This small band of pilots was ultimately responsible for the defense of their nation, and not only preserved their freedom and that of their countrymen, but gave Hitler his first major defeat of the war. In a speech to the House of Commons, Prime Minister Winston Churchill praised the pilots of the RAF, saying "If the British Empire and its Commonwealth last a thousand years, men will still say, 'this was their finest hour'."

The war was still far from over, and there was no certainty that the British would prevail. But the Battle of Britain proved to the world that Nazi tyranny was not victorious, there was still hope, and Great Britain was its brightest beacon.

Okey E. Taylor
December 8, 1924 -

Okey E. Taylor was born on December 8, 1924, in Clendenin, West Virginia, where he spent much of his childhood. When asked what he enjoyed most growing up, Okey loves to tell about the countless hours he and his friends spent playing any kind of game they could come up with. Games like Kick the Can, Hide and Seek, Basketball, and rubber gun battles were some of his personal favorites.

When the United States entered World War II, Okey, like millions of other young men, had to leave his home and family to join the fight. After basic training, Okey completed the five month course for the Army Specialized Training Program (ASTP). He then joined the 8th Armored Division stationed at Camp Polk, Louisiana.

The division first deployed to England and took up positions at Tidworth Barracks near Salisbury Plain. Then, in January of 1945, the unit deployed to the Metz-Nancy region in France to prevent a possible German breakthrough in the area. When he arrived with his division, Okey found himself in the middle of an intense and bloody battle that became known as the Colmar Pocket. Though the Allies suffered over 17,000 casualties, the heroism and determination of Okey and his comrades in arms broke the German attack and sent the enemy into retreat. On the heels of his first combat experience, Okey and his unit re-deployed to the Ardennes forest to join the last week of the Battle of the Bulge. Since they were primarily reserves, the unit saw little action, but though he

53

managed to dodge enemy fire, Okey did not escape the Bulge unscathed. The bitter cold of the winter caused him, like many other soldiers, to develop frostbitten feet. Fortunately, Okey made a swift recovery and rejoined his unit in time to participate in the final Allied push into Germany.

By crossing the Rhine River in March of 1945, the Allies had overcome the last natural barrier separating them from the German interior, but the battle was not yet over. Led by Adolf Hitler, the German military still refused to surrender. Okey and his division were one of many Allied units sent to capture the Ruhr, Germany's industrial region just east of the Rhine. After surrounding the area, the Allies began to slowly reduce the size of the pocket, as German forces surrendered or were overrun one by one. One day, while clearing the resistance in the eastern section of the pocket, Okey and his unit captured a German farmhouse situated on a small ridge. They found the farmer had a large storage area filled with dozens of eggs, along with several hams and a few loaves of German black bread. Having not eaten fresh eggs and ham in months, the men quickly set about cooking the food. The farmer was not at all happy to feed all these hungry American soldiers, but they ignored him. Just as they began to digest one of their better meals of the war, scouts reported a column of German tanks in the valley below. With full bellies, the men geared up for an attack. They called in air support from the fighters attached to their unit. To make sure they wouldn't be strafed by their own planes, the soldiers set up several 4 foot by 12 foot cerise-colored panels they carried with them. These panels reflected sunlight and could be seen for miles. This told the pilots where their friends were. However, Okey and his unit were clearing the eastern part of the Ruhr Pocket and were moving west; usually, it was the Germans to the East and the Allies to the west. The pilots had either forgotten or not been told of the situation and strafed east of the panels as they always had. Okey and the others ran for cover. Fortunately, no one was harmed; however, the platoon leader had not reached cover in time and one fighter's machine guns strafed on either side of him. Although he was not injured, coming within inches of death scared the wits out of him, and he was white as a sheet for some time afterward. After the incident, Okey felt a very slight bit of sympathy for the Germans (who were bombed and strafed daily) but still not much.

After clearing the Ruhr Pocket, Okey moved with his unit in their advance east, stopping only when they reached the Elbe River, the limit of the American advance. The rest of Germany was to be occupied by Soviets, although Okey's division could have advanced to Berlin if they were allowed too.

After the end of the war in Europe, Okey Taylor was ready to go home; he turned down a promotion to sergeant because it would have required him to remain in Europe for another six months. Arriving in New York City aboard a Victory ship on March 1, 1946, he was formally discharged on the 11th. Eager to get out of uniform, Okey had taken it off within five minutes after arriving home.

Over the next few months Okey did absolutely nothing besides throwing parties whenever a friend came home from Europe. However, the young man had to start a new life at some point, and he decided to go to college. He majored in mathematics and in 1951 began working for the Columbia Gas System. The company supplied natural gas to Ohio and six other eastern states for both residential and commercial customers. It also was one of the first companies to use computers. As early as 1958 Okey used computer programs to bill the two million gas customers. He used this experience later in his career to help design computers for other gas company operations.

Okey did not get married until he had finished college and saved some money. He married a woman named Patricia in 1958, and they had one son named Brad.

Okey is very proud of his service, proud that he was part of the greatest army in U.S. history, and that his generation turned America into a world class power. Unfortunately, he sees the generations after his (including mine) trying to turn it into a "Banana Republic." Okey's service is acknowledged with the medals and badges he received; The 8th Armored Division shoulder patch, the Combat Infantryman Badge, the Bronze Star, the Good Conduct Medal, the American Theatre ribbon, European Theatre of Operations ribbon, the German Occupation ribbon, and the World War II Victory ribbon.

Though proud of his service, Okey is saddened by the large number of men who were killed or wounded during the war. Two members of Okey's squad were killed and five wounded over the course of the campaign in Europe. The number in the whole company was higher. A number of his high school friends were also casualties in various battles around the world. One was wounded at Iwo Jima and woke up four months later at Bethesda Naval Hospital. The drum major in his high school band, who lived just two doors down from Okey, died in the Battle of the Bulge, and another friend was killed in North Africa. Okey's college roommate was wounded in Southern Germany.

If there is one thing Okey wants everyone to remember it is that freedom is not free. You only have rights if you have freedom, and you sometimes have to fight to keep them. Those who demand rights without assuming the responsibilities that go with them will soon have neither rights nor freedom. To sum this up, here is one of Okey's favorite quotes:

"They that can give up essential liberty to obtain a little temporary safety deserve neither liberty nor safety." - Benjamin Franklin, 1759

Paul Krouse

Paul Krouse was born in Delaware, Ohio and spent most of his childhood there. Because his father ran away from home when Paul was young, he and his brother were raised solely by their mother. Growing up, Paul loved to swim in the nearby river in his free time and made many great memories there.

After the Japanese attacked Pearl Harbor, Paul left his restaurant job in 1942 and went with a friend to enlist in the Navy. But they were both turned away because of color blindness and instead joined the Army. Because they loved tanks Paul and his friend were able to find positions in the newly formed 41st Cavalry Reconnaissance Squadron part of the 11th Armored Division in Camp Polk, Louisiana. While stationed there, they were constantly in training exercises, spending a full summer as part of the Third Army's huge Louisiana-Texas training maneuver. Then Paul and the rest of the division moved to Camp Barkeley, Texas in September and one month later relocated to Camp Ibis near Needles, California. The camp was in the Mojave Desert and the weather was brutal. The men trained in blazing hot days, slept in tents through bitter cold nights, and learned to deal with the sand that seemed to be everywhere. The desert tested both man and machine, but the Paul and the others held together and in February were moved again to Camp Cooke, California. Camp Cooke, situated on the coast with real barracks and bunks was much more comfortable than the desert. Training was still hard but after their time in the Mojave, nobody complained.

On September 17, 1944 Paul and the other men of the 11 Armored boarded railroad cars for a long four day journey to Camp Kilmer, New Jersey. There they remained for another week before boarding the U.S.S Hermitage for a voyage to England. Besides the occasional seasickness, the crossing for their convoy was peaceful and smooth, for they were fortunate enough to have no engine trouble or submarine attacks. After disembarking in Southampton, England on October 10, 1944 Paul's unit moved to Chippenham, England. But they would not be there for long.

On December 16, the Germans launched a massive offensive in the Ardennes forest, the Battle of the Bulge had begun. Three days later Paul and his comrades arrived in Cherbourg, France. They were supposed to assist in clearing out the Nazis besieged in the French town of Lorient, but with the brutal fighting in the Ardennes forest, reinforcements were desperately needed. The Paul and the rest of the 11th Armored nicknamed the "Thunderbolts" were to proceed immediately to the Meuse River and hold the line between the towns of Sedan and Givet. Paul's cavalry headed the area immediately, leaving the rest of the division in Cherbourg. They raced through the night to reach the frontline. When they arrived in the Ardennes area, the soldiers were sent to clear a nearby wood of Germans. During the following engagement a mortar hit Paul's friend and killed him. The loss crushed Paul. After the fight, he tried to distract himself by bringing up more ammunition.

For three weeks Paul fought alongside other American and British soldiers in the freezing cold and deep snow, all in an effort to eliminate the bulge and straiten the Allied line. By the second week of January the Germans were being forced back to their starting positions. The final phase of the battle would be characterized by the capture of the key town of Houffalize, Belgium on the Ourthe River, 10 miles north of Bagstone. The thunderbolt's attack began on January 13, but after two days of fighting, the town was still ten miles behind German lines.

In the Afternoon of January 15 the 41st was ordered to re-new the advance on Houffalize and make contact with the 2nd Armored Division, driving down from Achouffe. The push towards Houffalize proved to be long and difficult. The Germans put up a tough fight for the town Velleroux and after its capture Paul and the others had to advance to the village of Bonneure across a one-lane dirt road. By the time they had captured Bonneure night had fallen. But this didn't stop the men of the 41st. They advanced through the night in freezing cold weather and 18 inches of snow and by dawn could see Houffalize. They hoped to catch the Germans off guard, but were discovered before they could attack and a battle broke out. It wasn't until 9:05 A.M. when reinforcements from the 2nd Armored Division arrived, that the Americans were finally managed overwhelm the Germans and take the town.

After the Battle of the Bulge the Germans took up new positions along the Siegfried line in western Germany, preparing for a last ditch defense of the Fatherland. On February 26, the 41st sent patrols against the German positions. They broke through and by March 7 the squadron had captured the German town of Freringen and taken hundreds of prisoners. Paul and his companions then began advancing towards their next objective the Rhine River, the last natural obstacle between the Allies and the heart of Germany. But first they had to cross the Kyll, Moselle, and Nahe rivers to get there. They met almost no armed resistance; all that slowed them were road blocks and other obstacles, barricading the roads. After crossing the first two rivers the squadron reached the town of Herrstein and captured a group of Germans attempting to setting up a road block. They then moved to Fischbach with plans to capture a bridge over the Nahe. But the Germans blew the bridge before the Americans got there.

Although the Germans blew the bridge, the Americans managed to find a suitable crossing point. Once across the Nahe the thunderbolts continued to the Rhine. They seized the towns of Hundsbach and Breitenheim, shot up two enemy columns, took large amounts of equipment, and more than 1,000 prisoners. After this Paul and the rest of the 41st triumphantly crossed the Rhine and participated in the "rat race" across Germany. They rarely ran into strong resistance and most Germans surrendered without a fight. The main task became moving road blocks and repairing blown bridges as the squadron advanced through Germany and into Austria. After the capture of Linz, patrols were sent out to make contact with the Russians who were approaching from the east. On the first day, no Russians were found, but one patrol sent out discovered the Nazi concentration camp at Mauthausen and all of its grim atrocities. Bones and dead bodies were everywhere and the survivors bone thin. The smell was so bad that people in the town could smell it. This is why Paul and the others don't believe the civilian claims that they didn't know about the 'camp'. Soldiers tried to help by giving the prisoners food. But they gave too much and the severely underfed prisoners got sick or died from being overfed, greatly upsetting

Paul. The 41st first contact with the Russians didn't go as planned, because Russian fighters overhead mistook them for the enemy and strafed them. But on May 8, 1945, the day the war ended, the Americans linked up with Russian ground troops.

After the surrender of Germany, Paul took up a position in Bayreuth, Germany. To return home he has to get enough points on the Army point system. Points were earned by the amount of time overseas, amount of time in the army, or if you were married. To earn enough points, meant Paul had to stay on occupation duty in Germany. While there he met and fell in love with a young German woman, but wasn't allowed to bring her to America. After he received enough points, Paul signed up for another three months in Germany hoping the rules would change and he could take her home with him. But it didn't happen, when his three months were up, Paul bid a sad farewell and began the long trip home.

Corporal Paul Krouse returned to the states on March 7, 1946 and before doing anything else, went out and got drunk.

Paul's service and bravery is recognized by the medals he received. The Ardennes, Rhineland, and Central Europe with 3 battle stars.

The day he was discharged, Paul joined the army reserve and in 1947 transferred to the National Guard. Paul married Ruth Ann Shaw on October 11, 1946. They had 5 children, Suzanna, Karen, Melinda, Denise, and Stephen. Although he was recalled to fight in Korea, Paul instead ended up back in Germany, as part of the 175th Military Police Battalion. After returning home a second time, he became a captain for the City of Delaware's Police Department in 1950. Paul remained on the force until he retired in 1979 at the age 54. In his retirement

Paul has managed to do two of things he always wanted to do, travel the world and buy Harley motorcycle, one of his most prized possessions.

He also spends lots of time with his family, which now includes 12 grandchildren and 11 great-grandchildren.

In reflecting on his service, Paul is very proud to be an American. But with that pride, is a sadness for the loss of many friends during the war.

William (Bill) Ruth
May 18, 1922 -

William (Bill) Ruth was born on May 18, 1922, in Johnstown, Pennsylvania, where he grew up. He learned many things from the hard depression and seeing many adults out of work. Although his family had little money, they were 'rich' in memories. Most of these memories came from the activities they did together.

Bill left his home and family for the military on December 2, 1942. After a sad farewell, Bill boarded the train and left. Bill spent a week on that train, traveling across the United States to Camp Beule in California. When he arrived, Bill had to take a medical exam. After the exam, the doctor sent him to the hospital for surgery. At the hospital, Bill caught a bad cold. It took a full month before he was strong enough to have surgery. Behind in training, Bill had to work hard to catch up. He managed to do it, and then became a tank crewman for the Service Company of the 46 Armored Regiment, part of the 13 Armored Division. The division left Camp Beule for Camp Bowie, Texas, during the December of 1943. Unfortunately they did not get the warm-weather break they had expected. They found temperatures as low as 20 degrees. This came as a shock to those who had always viewed Texas as warm all year-round. Bill spent less than three weeks in Texas before he was sent to radio school in Fort Knox, Kentucky. There he was trained as a radio operator and was able to rejoin his unit in Camp Bowie when he graduated in April 1944. He remained there for just one short month until he was transferred to a replacement unit and boarded a train that was headed for the coast. On May 18, Bill's 22nd birthday, the train passed through his hometown in Pennsylvania. He suddenly got very homesick. He knew it could be a while before he saw his family again. He wished the train would stop in Johnstown. Bill's wish was granted when the train stopped. He quickly found a pencil and paper, wrote a quick note, and threw it out the nearest open window and hoped someone would pick it up and contact his parents. In fact, Bill was given a furlough a few days later and learned that a man named Homer Shaeffer had delivered the note to his father. Bill kept the note.

Every soldier ever sent to war knows the pain and sadness of saying goodbye to their family and friends, and the uncertainty of not knowing if they will see them again. Bill found it hard to say goodbye to his loved ones, as he knew it could be years before they saw each other again. He felt relieved when Johnstown disappeared from sight and the ordeal was over.

Bill arrived at Camp Miles Standish, Massachusetts, on May 28; four days later, he boarded the U.S. Mount Vernon and headed for England the very next day. It took 11 days for the convoy to reach England. It suffered no losses, but the ships did fire depth charges on June 6, which raised the fear of a submarine attack.

After his arrival in England, Bill spent his first few days at "Camp Embro" and then moved to Camp Barwick. There, the men trained for fighting in the hedges and marshes of Normandy, where most of the fighting was currently happening. Bill enjoyed his stay at Camp Barwick. He made new friends and was able to visit the nearby town of Yeovil. The food was good, and the men slept in huts that had plumbing instead of tents. On July 17, the men packed their gear and took a two-mile hike with all 75 pounds of gear on their backs. They then boarded a train to the town of Brockenhust outside Southampton. After another long, two-mile hike in the July heat they arrived at another camp, where they received live ammunition -- a clear sign they were heading to France. That night they boarded a landing craft that took them across the English Channel.

On July 18, 1944, Bill landed on Omaha Beach after a short voyage across the English Channel. Bill remembers clearly what he saw when he stepped off the boat: the craters in the hill to their right, destroyed tanks, smashed rifles, and the graves of dead soldiers. A group of German POWs (Prisoners of War) boarded the boat he and his comrades had just quitted. He envied them because they were headed for the safety of a POW camp, while he and his friends were off to fight the Germans who had not given up.

Bill experienced many amazing and sad things while in France. On the morning of July 25, one week after his arrival, Bill awoke to the sound of bombers and their fighter escorts. These bombers and fighter escorts were flying to bomb the German positions at St. Lo. Three Thousand planes flew over Bill and his comrades' heads all day. They were flying from England to drop their bombs then flying back to reload. It was as if there was a two lane road in the sky with planes going in both directions. Bill would also come under occasional bombing and strafing during the summer and fall of 1944 when the Luftwaffe was still at large. During his time in the replacements, Bill traveled through many liberated cities and towns. Some, like the city of St. Lo, shocked him because of the extent of their devastation. However, as the German armies retreated faster, the damage in towns or the number of destroyed vehicles reduced. On August 13, Bill was taken out of the replacements and joined the 33 Armored Regiment part of the 3rd Armored Division.

During the fight for France, Bill, along with his unit, got lost in woods and had to live off Mother Nature for three days until another unit found them. On the way back, they took a wrong turn and ended up in a town still occupied by the Germans. Bullets started flying, and the Americans had to scramble for cover. Desperate for cover, Bill spotted a brick wall – ten to twelve feet high – that would give him cover if he could get over it. Despite the seventy-five pounds of gear on his back, Bill managed to get up and over the wall. Although they were the underdog, the American infantrymen held their positions until their tanks arrived to push the Germans out of town. After this incident, Bill and his Third Armored were part of the lead American soldiers. They were even ahead of the reconnaissance units. As they advanced through French and Belgian towns, they met snipers that had been left behind by the retreating German armies to slow the Allied advance. On September 2, Bill and his comrades crossed the border into Belgium and approached the town of Mons. Just as in other towns, snipers delayed them. Bill and another soldier had to hide in a nearby barn, but a sniper found them and fired at them with a machine gun. One bullet just missed Bill and hit the other soldier in the leg. Once the men located the sniper and took him out with a bazooka, the medics evacuated the soldier with the other wounded. Bill often wondered what happened to this wounded soldier, but never saw or heard from him again.

As the Allies continued into Belgium, as they liberated more cities and towns, the Belgians greeted them enthusiastically. One family even made breakfast for Bill and his buddies. Since they needed a new radio operator,

Bill was reassigned to the regiment's service company. It came as a relief; he had been worried because he knew the reconnaissance company needed replacements, too, and they had 400% casualties, which meant every position in the company had been filled by a replacement four times. Bill learned that the reason the service company had selected him was the commanders were big baseball fans, and seeing his last name Ruth, decided he must be a baseball player. After joining the company, Bill was always addressed as George Herman. Even today, at reunions he is still addressed by this nickname. He also learned that the man he replaced, Joe Michael, from Chicago, had been killed in a half-track by a German tank when they took a wrong turn near Liege, Belgium. On September 12, the men of the 3rd Armored Division crossed the border and captured the town of Roetgen, the first German town to fall to the Allies. As they drove through town, Bill noticed there were no applauding crowds. Instead the people lining the streets just stood and watched the Americans go by. White sheets, signaling surrender, were hung in the windows of houses and buildings. A week later, the division stopped at Breinig, Germany to rest, repair vehicles, and get desperately needed supplies. Bill and his buddies remained there for the next three months. Although the Germans made no attempt to retake the town, the artillery and aerial bombardment was constant. Six men were killed by the bombardment during the unit's time in Breinig. Bill could tell whenever he saw the face of a German civilian that they, too, wanted the war to be brought to an end.

When the German offensive in the Ardennes opened on December 16, Bill and the others were told to pack and be ready to leave at a moment's notice. They moved out four days later in the middle of the night. The

darkness and fog limited visibility, and the muddy roads
stalled their movement. On Christmas Eve the men
stopped in Spa, Belgium. To celebrate Christmas, the
cooks made turkey and brought out bottles of
Champagne at around midnight. While they were
celebrating, the battalion commander radioed them to
move out to counter a German attack. But most men
drank too much and could not perform their duties. The
captain had no choice but to tell the commander they
could not help. They were given till 4 A.M. to shape up.
They were ready on time, but then were told to stay, when
another tank company stopped the advancing Germans.

During the next month, the company was
constantly on the move. They stayed with Belgian
families and had to avoid artillery shells. Although his
company did not engage in combat, Bill was injured, but
not in battle. He received a hug from the Warrant
Officer, who accidentally broke two of his ribs. This
forced him to leave his unit for more than a week until he
recovered.

The company set out for Germany on the 6th of
February, 1945. They assembled at the town of Busbach,
Germany. They waited for the final offensive in to
Germany to be launched. Instead, the Germans opened
the Roer dams and flooded the area. It wasn't until
February 28 that the Americans were able to cross the
river. After the crossing, Bill fought to liberate many
German towns and cities. Every town he went through
was destroyed. As they worked their way toward the
Rhine River, Bill did not see a single civilian. Whole towns
were often deserted with few exceptions. In the town of
Berrendorf, Bill recalls such exception as five hundred
civilians waited in a church to surrender to the Americans.
When he entered the German city of Cologne on March

8, Bill made a very interesting discovery. Ford Motor Company had a plant there before the war, and, despite the fact that the whole town had been turned to rubble by the Allied air campaign, the plant remained untouched.

After crossing the famous Rhine River, the 3rd Armored Division advanced deep into Germany. Many towns surrendered without a fight, but some Germans, in towns like Marburg and Paderborn, fought fanatically to the bitter end. This slowed but did not stop the Allies. Many Allied soldiers found themselves greeted and cheered on by Allied POWs who had been forced into bone-breaking labor during the war. Many Germans finally began realizing the war was a lost cause. This was clearly expressed when, while using the bathroom in the woods, Bill was astonished to have three German soldiers walk to him and surrendered. All alone and unable to defend himself, the Germans could easily have killed him, but instead waited for him to finish his current task and then handed over their weapons. Proving, for probably the sixth time that Bill was destined to live a long life.

While he stood Guard duty on May 8, 1945, Bill learned the news the whole world had waited for, Germany had surrendered. With no more killing or shooting or destruction and fear, a huge burden was lifted off the soldiers fighting in Europe and their families at home.

Over the next few months, Bill watched as his friends began to head for home. He waited patiently for the time when he would have enough points. To pass time, he took up the job as regimental ration sergeant. He had to work many hours, but it was better than sitting around wishing he was home. Finally, after six months of waiting and delays, Bill finally boarded the U.S.S Hermitage on November 23, and arrived home eight days later. Two days after his arrival, he was decommissioned, and his family came in his car to pick him up. They cried as they embraced and were happy to be together again. Bill at last came home to the house, town, and people he had missed so much.

During his first months home, Bill struggled to remember he wasn't in a war zone anymore. He kept looking at possible places to hide from enemy fire and tried not to duck while driving. Bill used his G.I. Bill to pay for college. He attended Pennsylvania State University and majored in Agriculture. He then taught Agriculture at several schools in Pennsylvania and Westerville, Ohio. Bill married Eulalia Mary Conway on June 12, 1948, and together they had 5 children. They also currently have 12 grandchildren and 3 great-grandchildren.

Bill is most proud to have answered the call of duty and to have seen the patriotism of all Americans. But he is saddened by the death of so many people on both sides over the course of the war.

The Attack of the Rising Sun

"TORA! TORA! TORA!", JAPANESE FOR Tiger, this is the coded message Mitsuo Fuchida sent back to the waiting Japanese fleet as his plane broke through the clouds and saw the American base at Pearl Harbor. With that, Fuchida took his Zero fighter into a dive. Following his lead, the other Japanese pilots descended from the sky. The attack on Pearl Harbor had begun.

Fuchida's message was the signal to the Japanese commanders that the Americans were unprepared, and complete surprise had been achieved. The day was December 7, 1941, a date that is forever burned into the American mind. The United States, which had so far managed to refrain from being dragged into the war in Europe, was suddenly delivered a devastating blow from an enemy on the other side of the planet. In that single morning, over 2,000 Americans would die, and more than 1,000 would be injured. Americans who had woken to a normal, peaceful Sunday would fall asleep to the thoughts of the tragedy that had befallen the nation, and the clouds of war that loomed ahead.

Since the outbreak of war in Europe, the United States had remained neutral. The country was dominated by an isolationist mindset. Many Americans saw no reason to become involved in foreign wars whose outcome, they believed, did not affect the United States. President Franklin Roosevelt, however, did not share their views. He saw Hitler as the threat he was, and did not think the Atlantic Ocean would be enough to protect America from the dangers of a Nazi Europe. Even though America remained officially neutral, Roosevelt felt compelled to do what he could to aid the British in their fight against Hitler. He loaned them US destroyers and had US factories supply England with tanks, aircraft, and other munitions of war. The isolationists opposed all of these moves, fearing the Germans would use Roosevelt's actions as a pretext to declare war on the United States. Indeed, German submarines did attack and sink several US destroyers that would escort British ships in American waters. But the sinkings were not enough reason for the public or Congress to go to war with Germany.

Ultimately, despite the fears of being dragged into the conflict in Europe, it would be the Japanese, not the Germans, who brought the United States into the Second World War.

Frustrated by Japan's refusal to stop its aggressive attacks into China and Southeast Asia, in July of 1941 Roosevelt cut off all oil exports to the island nation. Because Japan relied on the United States for nearly 80% of its oil, it would not be long before the Empire would run dry and all military operations would halt. Roosevelt had backed Japan into a corner; either the country must halt its conquests of Asia and begin negotiations with China, or its military machine would wither away.

Far from starting the peace process, the oil embargo on Japan began the countdown to war between the Empire and America. The Japanese government leaders were adamant. Japan would continue its righteous expansion in Asia and the Pacific. If they could not rely on trade with the United States for oil and other war materials, they would acquire them through conquest. The Japanese believed they could not seize the resources they needed to become a self-sufficient nation without the United States intervening at some point. They therefore decided to launch a preemptive strike to knock America out of the war before it had a chance to enter. The man charged with the heavy responsibility of planning and executing an attack that could achieve this daring objective was Admiral Isoroku Yamamoto.

The plan that Yamamoto drafted was as unprecedented as it was daring. The plan called for a series of coordinated attacks on the Dutch East Indies, the British colony Malaya, and the American-controlled Philippines. This would be followed by the seizure of other key Pacific islands. The goal; to seize the natural resources Japan needed and use the Pacific islands as bases to defend the newly claimed territory. All these attacks had to be made by amphibious landing, and to ensure the landings' success, the Japanese would need control of the seas, meaning the US Pacific Fleet had to be eliminated. Stationed at Pearl Harbor in Oahu, Hawaii, the Pacific fleet consisted of three aircraft carriers, eight battle ships, and dozens of smaller ships. The primary targets for this surprise attack would be the aircraft carriers and their aircraft. The Japanese would also destroy the battleships, as many smaller vessels as possible, and the land-based planes on Oahu.

On November 26, six aircraft carriers and their escort ships, under the command of Admiral Chuichi Nagumo, sailed from Japan and began the 4,000 mile journey to Hawaii. It would take twelve days for the fleet to reach its attack position. In the meantime, complete radio silence was enforced to ensure the Americans did not pick up any signals. Fake radio traffic created a phantom fleet in another area of the Pacific. In Washington, D.C., Japanese diplomats continued to pretend to negotiate terms for a possible withdrawal from China in exchange for an end to the US oil embargo. Even though their government no longer considered negotiation an option, this deceptive diplomacy would continue right up until the first bombs were dropped on Oahu.

At dawn on the morning of December 7, 1941, one hundred and eighty-three planes bearing the infamous symbol of the rising sun took off from six aircraft carriers and assembled into formation. These aircraft were the primary strike force, the first of three waves that were to hit the American positions on Oahu. Led by Captain Mitsuo Fuchida, they were to destroy the American air force on the islands and cripple the ships in Pearl Harbor. The second and third waves would then follow to destroy any remaining targets and render the American navy incapacitated for the foreseeable future. But as the Japanese pilots prepare for their approach on Hawaii, there is a problem. Japanese spies on Oahu now report that the American aircraft carriers, the primary targets of the attacks, aren't there. The objective to annihilate the Pacific fleet is impossible to achieve with the Americans' most powerful ships out at sea. But the attack cannot be delayed; it is supposed to be synchronized with offensives elsewhere. Admiral Nagumo ordered Captain Fuchida to proceed as planned. As the first wave approached Oahu from the North and East. It was picked up on American radar. When informed of the unidentified aircraft, the American officer at the station assumed from the direction the planes were coming that it was the B-17 bombers that were supposed to arrive from the mainland that day. It would be a terrible mistake.

December 7th, started as an average, peaceful Sunday morning. In the harbor, many sailors were sleeping in and taking it easy. Others were spending the weekend on shore leave, enjoying the tropical luxuries found only in Hawaii. The quiet tranquility vanished in the blink of an eye, when, at 7:55, Japanese planes broke through the beautiful white clouds, began their attack dive, and all hell broke loose.

With the aircraft carriers out of port, the eight battleships, the pride of the American fleet, became the main Japanese target. Moored along Battleship Row, the ships could not have been more vulnerable. Torpedo bombers dove low to release their payload, while dive bombers screamed overhead. The battleships Oklahoma and Tennessee were ripped open by torpedoes and began to sink; the California ignited into a fireball that reached 500 feet when it's arsenal was hit. The Arizona exploded when a bomb hit the forward magazine, causing an explosion that blew the ship apart, sinking it in minutes and taking 1,177 crew members with it.

The confused and disorganized American sailors scrambled to fight back, sometimes even using hammers to smash the locks on ammunition boxes and then rushing with as much ammo as they could carry to their posts. Sailors on shore leave rushed back to their ships to help, even swimming when necessary. But fighting back became increasingly difficult as more ships were hit and began to sink. Some had to be abandoned, with men jumping into water thick with burning oil that had leaked from sinking ships. While the main Japanese strike force focused on Pearl Harbor, other formations dealt with the two American airbases on Oahu. When thinking of a Japanese attack, American commanders had envisioned small groups or individuals sabotaging their aircraft. To prevent this, they had all planes parked side by side along the runway. This made them easy to guard from saboteurs, but unfortunately it made them easy targets for the Japanese pilots. Three hundred and forty-three aircraft would be destroyed or damaged during the Japanese attack, almost all of them during the first wave. As Fuchida's planes withdrew, they left behind unimaginable destruction-hundreds of planes lay in ruin, dozens of ships sinking, hundreds of men dead or dying.

But it wasn't over. Just like a hurricane after a brief break, the Japanese storm returned in full force. The second wave, another 171 Japanese aircraft, hit Oahu, attacking any survivors of the first attack. The second wave did not fare as well as the first. By now the element of surprise was gone, and the Americans were ready. Heavy antiaircraft fire blanketed the sky, making it difficult for the pilots to hit a target without getting shot down. But this did not stop the Japanese from sinking several ships and causing additional destruction to the already beleaguered Americans. Ninety minutes after the first bombs were dropped, it was over. The harbor fell silent again, this time permanently, as the Japanese fleet began to withdraw. Due to increased American resistance during the second wave, and unsure how close the American carriers were, Nagumo decided not to launch the planned third strike, believing the damage done to be sufficient.

As the Japanese plowed through the calm waters of the Pacific back to Japan, back on Oahu the entire island was in chaos. Unaware of the Japanese withdrawal men continued to prepare and man new defenses. Fear and uncertainty ran through every man and woman. Was another Japanese wave inbound to appear in the sky at any moment? Were the airstrikes a prelude to a full-scale invasion of Oahu? Were Japanese saboteurs already on the island preparing to cause more damage to their already crippled defenses? The anxiety and confusion led to many tragic accidents on that terrible day. Hawaiian civilians who had witnessed the destruction of the Japanese attack and rushed to Pearl Harbor to help were shot by nervous guards. Patrols spent the day scouting the beaches looking for a nonexistent invasion fleet. Some were still out when darkness fell, and in the confusion of the night, two American patrols opened fire on each other. In the harbor itself, while there was no longer any shooting, many lives were still endangered. Sailors struggled to save sinking ships. Those that were abandoned had crew in water thick with burning oil. The battleship Oklahoma had flipped upside down and slowly began to sink. With most of the ship's crew trapped inside, rescue teams began a desperate effort to cut through the hull before their comrades ran out of oxygen.

As news of the attack spread across the country, the nation was driven into shock. How could this have happened? How could the United States be caught so off guard? What would happen next? The third question was the first to be answered as the Japanese began their invasions of the Philippines, the Dutch East Indies, and other islands in the south Pacific.

Even as darkness fell over Pearl Harbor, it could not hide the destruction that stretched as far as one could see. Wounded and dying men lay in pain in hospitals and makeshift medical facilities; crews continued to patch up holes on sinking ships; rescue teams continued to cut through the hull of the Oklahoma in a desperate attempt to save their comrades trapped inside. Two-thousand, four hundred and two American servicemen were dead, another one thousand, one hundred and forty-three injured, and nearly a hundred civilians killed or wounded. eighteen ships, including all eight battleships were sunk or seriously damaged, and over 200 planes put out of commission. The U.S. could no longer protect its other Pacific territories, many of which were already under attack. With no support or reinforcements available to the American and Allied positions in the region, many of these islands quickly fell into Japanese hands.

The Japanese strike on Pearl Harbor appeared to have succeeded, but it had not. Though the damage is extensive, the Japanese failed to eliminate the threat the Americans at Oahu pose. They did not destroyed US fuel depots, and left the dry-dock facilities intact, allowing the Americans to begin the rebuilding and rearming process almost immediately. The Japanese did not target the US submarine base on the island, and this would prove key to the American victory in the Pacific, as the submarine fleet would sever supply lines to many of the new Japanese territories, and slowly starve the island nation.

And though the battleships, the pride of the American fleet, lay burning and sinking, the day of the battleship was over before Pearl Harbor. Aircraft carriers now command the seas, and these ships had eluded the destruction of Pearl Harbor, and continued to pose a threat to the Japanese control of the Pacific.

Across America the initial shock turned into burning rage as the reality of the Japanese attack sank in. Isolationism, long held as the dominant political ideology, disappeared overnight. As President Roosevelt addressed Congress, asking for a declaration of war, recruitment stations in every part of the country were overwhelmed by swarms of men rushing to enlist.

The Japanese had planned the attack at Pearl Harbor to be a severe blow to public morale and believed it would break their will to fight a lengthy war. But far from the breaking the American will, the Japanese had actually created the will to join the war. The sleeping giant had awakened, and he was looking for a fight.

Paul (Gene) Kohli
May 5 1923 -

Paul (Gene) Kohli was born on May 5, 1923, and raised on the eighty- acre family farm in Pandora, Ohio. Although growing up in the Great Depression proved harsh, his loving and understanding parents and brother, combined with their strong Christian values, eased the mind even in the face of great hardships.

After graduating from high school in 1941, Gene got a job at Tripleh Electrical Instrument Company, working long hours from 5PM to 1AM to pay off college bills. Many nights while working late Gene would often see two Japanese students come out of the campus and ride off on their bikes. They would be gone for hours at a time. He never did find out where they went or what they did, but became more suspicious when on December 5th, 1941, the two Japanese students disappeared, leaving all their belongings behind. Two days later, Japan attacked Pearl Harbor and America entered the Second World War.

Gene received his draft notice in 1942 and went to Camp Perry in March 1943 to take a psychological exam. The test was taken by selecting one of the multiple answers and punching a hole in the paper with your choice. Then it was graded by lining up the holes to the answer key. If you received enough points, you were somehow qualified for Officer Candidate School. Gene had to be hunched over the paper in a freezing room for hours during the exam, and in the end he missed officer school by just two points and ended up at Camp Shelby, Mississippi. There he joined Company C, part of the

202nd Combat Engineer Battalion, as a jeep driver. One time the whole company lined up and anyone with truck driving experience was told to step forward. Although he did have experience, Gene remembered to avoid the temptation to step forward. He could hear his father's voice telling him "don't volunteer for anything unless you know what you're volunteering for." He didn't step forward, and the volunteers got to eat first, then were given wheelbarrows and put to work.

When the company was in bivouac, Gene decided to go to the nearby town of Keeslerfield in Biloxi, Mississippi, to see his cousins. His friend Sergeant Skuta also had a friend in town, and the two decided to leave together. To leave camp, they had to have a trip ticket that had a jeep number on it. But they had the wrong tickets and were arrested by the guard, who thought it was a stolen vehicle and locked them in the guard house. They had to call the platoon commander to get out and were disappointed when Gene didn't get to see his cousins or Skuta's friend.

When his company arrived at Camp Miles Standish, the rain was pouring down. They all had to stand in a long hallway, but didn't know why. Their only hint was the doctors and nurses near the front, working their way down the line of soldiers. Gene's friend, Ferdy Sandfoss, was nervous because he didn't know what the doctors were going to do. His answer came without warning and in a form he probably didn't like, when a doctor and a nurse approached him, pulled back has raincoat, swabbed his butt, and jabbed him with a needle. Ferdy was so shocked he fainted with a 'full bladder' and as Gene put it, "took a leak in the hall." When Ferdy woke up, he didn't remember the event at all. Gene felt the need to tell his friend about his accident but had trouble explaining such a...unique situation.

Sent to Boston later in 1943, the battalion boarded the Santa Elena, destined for Liverpool. Once onboard, Gene and a few other soldiers received orders to report to the stern of the ship. Due to his lack of experience with ships, he had to ask for directions to the stern. When he arrived a sergeant handed him a hose and ordered him to wash off all the garbage on the back of the ship into the sea. The smell of garbage proved so disgusting, intoxicating, and overwhelming, it made Gene sick. Even after the garbage had been removed, the toxic smell remained. The sick feeling Gene got in the first hours of his voyage would linger for the full seventeen-day journey across the Atlantic. The smell on C deck, where Gene slept, was as bad as the garbage on the stern. Fortunately he soon discovered a way to avoid the stench when wanting to go to sleep. Before heading down to C deck, Gene would inhale as much fresh sea air as his lungs could hold, run to his bunk as fast as he possibly could, and get horizontal before taking another breath.

Since there were 3,500 men onboard, and only 1,500 bunks, each man had a card that told him when he could eat and sleep. With the stench of garbage almost everywhere, the food served onboard certainly didn't ease the stomach. Each man had two meals a day, twelve hours apart. Gene's meals were at 2AM and 2PM. The cooks often just grabbed whatever edible substances they found in the cans and cooked it. This didn't help the seasickness, and Gene spent 36 hours of the trip sitting on or kneeling over a toilet, which was actually just a pipe on the ship's rail with a toilet seat on it. Since he had only one canteen of water per day, he was often dehydrated, and decided after learning from some of his buddies' experiences to not take a salt water shower. After days of misery due to seasickness Gene found a cure by eating olives and a giant pickle. After that meal he amazingly did not get seasick again.

After a stop at Liverpool, England, the men boarded another ship for Northern Ireland. The Irish people showed their support for the Allied cause by warmly welcoming the soldiers when they arrived and set up camp. After dropping off Gene and the soldiers, the Santa Elena headed for the Mediterranean, where it would be sunk by a German torpedo plane on its very next mission. Besides having only holes with shacks over them, and many of the men getting diarrhea, life at camp proved much better than on the ship, until the unit suffered its first casualties. The battalion major ordered a minefield to be laid, with the pins pulled to make it realistic. Nobody knew why the major issued the order, for there weren't any hostiles in Ireland. But the real danger came when the same major ordered the mines to be removed by picking them up and reinserting the pins. Three men were assigned the dangerous task. One little mistake would lead to their deaths. One man did make a mistake, and no one knows exactly what happened, but he most likely inserted the wrong pin, setting off the mine and those stacked next to it. All three men vanished in the blink of an eye, with no remains left, not even dog tags. Another soldier in the unit walked the major out of camp that tragic evening. He returned a while later, but the major was never seen again. At a reunion years later, Gene found the courage to ask the man what happened to the major. "I'm not going to tell you or anybody else" he responded "Don't ever ask that question again."

Gene's stay in Northern Ireland was marked by another sad event. Early one foggy morning, Gene and a group of soldiers were on guard duty, watching the cinder path that ran by camp. While they stood watch, a local Irish man walking six racer dogs came into view. As he walked by camp, the dogs detected a rabbit nearby and ran in that direction. Since the man had the leashes tied around his hands, the dogs pulled him off balance and dragged him face-first along the cinder road. Gene and the soldiers were humored by the event, until the man managed to get back up and they saw what the cinders had done to face, arms, and legs. "I thought it was funny until I saw his face. After that it wasn't funny anymore," Gene would later say. He offered to take him to the medics in camp, but the man walked off without saying a word. They didn't see him again.

Gene's unit deployed to Southhampton, England next, where they were loaded on a ship to be part of the Normandy landings. They spent the days before D-day floating in the channel waters. One day while alone, they got close enough to the French coast that they could see the beaches. The Germans could certainly see them, too, but made no attempt to engage. Later the ship ran out of fuel and had to be towed back to port.

Gene landed in Normandy shortly after the initial attack on June 6, 1944. The night after the landings, Gene saw a sight he would never forget: a group of six trucks filled with dead Americans covered by their nation's flag. As they drove by, Paul realized he could have been one of those soldiers. It is a thought that never left him.

During the fight for France, Gene and Sergeant Skuta captured and boarded a docked German submarine. Inside the sub, the men found the stoves hot and food still warm, evidence that the Germans had left just minutes before their arrival. The most interesting discovery would have been steaks sent by German supporters in Argentina. Gene and Skuta grabbed as many as they could and took them back to the rest of their unit. The men enjoyed steaks for the next couple of days until a senior officer found out and ordered them to bury the rest since it wasn't US Army issue, much to everyone's annoyance.

After the breakthrough at St. Lo, Gene was driving the captain's jeep in the company's convoy, when they were forced to stop at an intersection because of a huge crater in the middle of it. The vehicles were parked bumper-to-bumper, making them a vulnerable target to a German attack. Then a new jeep approached the convoy, with the passenger standing up, holding the windshield for support. When it stopped, General George Patton himself stepped down. He gave Paul's company commander quite a scolding for having the convoy parked in such a vulnerable way and then drove forward. But his jeep got stuck in the crater when they tried to drive through it. Gene and his buddies worked quickly to pull it out, making him one of the few men who could say they lifted General Patton's jeep out of a crater.

Stationed in Stavelot, Belgium, when the Battle of the Bulge began, Gene's unit redeployed to reinforce the beleaguered Americans fighting in the Ardennes. On one freezing cold night Gene and Sergeant Skuta were on a night patrol, when they were challenged by an American soldier who thought they were Germans in disguise. They were ordered to throw down their weapons and report to his command post for questioning. They were soon released and learned the soldier had been in Europe for less than 48 hours and was suspicious because both Gene and Skuta spoke English a second language, because Skuta had learned Polish as a child and Gene learned Swiss-German.

Later, Gene and Sergeant Skuta went on another patrol, this time in daylight. While they were inspecting water points and a local fuel dump, the silence suddenly shattered as gunfire broke out nearby. From their experience, it didn't sound like a firefight which confused them. Gene later learned the shooting was the Malmendy Massacre, where about ninety Americans were killed because the Germans didn't want to care for the prisoners.

Although not shot during the Battle of the Bulge, Gene did not come out of the Battle of the Bulge in full health. Like many Allied soldiers, he suffered from frostbitten feet, but managed to make a full recovery.

By April 1945, Germany had been all but defeated, and Gene's attention increasingly turned to his stomach, as he got a strong craving for popcorn. He sent a letter home requesting his family send him some. His parents kindly sent their son a sealed can of popcorn. Knowing the Germans would surrender soon, Gene decided to keep it hidden until they did. May 8, 1945, the day after Germany surrendered, proved a day worth celebrating, and Gene provided the food. As the men began to devour the popcorn, a group of hungry German children came running from their homes, and the soldiers invited them to join their victory meal.

Corporal Gene Kohli returned home in early December 1945. After spending the years away from family and in the horror of war, Gene's emotions reached a climax as the ship passed the Statue of Liberty. Thinking of the sacrifices made by millions of men and women around the world, he cried unashamedly as he passed the ultimate symbol of America freedom. As soon as he disembarked at Pier #46 in Manhattan, New York, Gene headed for a delicatessen shop and bought a whole pecan pie and a quart of milk for himself, eating every crumb and drinking all the milk. He remembers this as one of the highlights of his first months back home.

Thankful and happy to be back with his family, Gene began his postwar life. He married his fiancé, Marcele, on April 20, 1946, at St. John Mennonite Church in Pandora, Ohio. The couple had two daughters, Candace and Karis. Their family has expanded over the years to include four grandchildren, and one granddaughter-in-law.

Gene held a number of jobs after leaving the military, working as a junior high school teacher, coach, counselor, and assistant principal for 17 years and as wedding photographer until he retired in 1983. Two years later he came out of retirement to work as a test administrator for the Office of Personnel and Management and the Department of Defense, where he still works part time.

Gene's service was acknowledged by the medals he received-the Good Conduct Medal, Battle of the Bulge campaign medal, and four others.

He takes no pride in his WWII service; he just tried to be a good soldier. The saddest part of his service is the loss of some close friends during training and combat.

Gene wants everyone to remember that the Allies prevented the Germans from doing what they so badly wanted to do. They thought we would be a pushover and easy to defeat, but we didn't allow that to happen, thank God!

Richard Lee Lynam

August 25, 1923 – January 5, 1945

Richard Lee Lyman was born on August 25, 1923 in Columbus, Ohio and grew up in the surrounding towns of Linworth and Worthington.

Richard received his draft notice in 1941, sadly leaving his loving family; he took a train to Fort Benning, Georgia to prepare for the dangerous life as a paratrooper. After training he joined the 517th Parachute Infantry Regiment, attached to the 11th Airborne in Camp McCall North Carolina. The 517th deployed to Italy in May 1944. After several months there Richard moved with his unit to France in August. When the German offensive opened in the Ardennes Richard was in Bergeval, Belgium. Sent to stop the German breakthrough, he fought bravely alongside his fellow Americans in the bitter cold and blazing heat of battle, until he made the ultimate sacrifice on January 5, 1945. He was 21 years old.

For his service and sacrifice Richard Lee Lynam posthumously received the Silver Star, the Bronze Star, and three Purple Hearts.

This page honors the life of a true American soldier, gone but not forgotten. May Private Richard Lynam's sacrifice never be forgotten and may his story be a lasting tribute to all the service men and women who gave their lives, to protect ours.

Lawrence Bott
December 23, 1924 -

Born in Union Town,
Pennsylvania, on December 23,
1924, Lawrence Bott was the
second of five children. As a
young child, his father's job took the family to Columbus,
Ohio. But when his grandparents fell ill, Lawrence and his
family moved back to Pennsylvania to care for them.
They lived on his grandparents' farm until their death in
1935. The Bott family then moved back to Columbus.

On May 31, 1943, two weeks before his high
school graduation, Lawrence received orders to report to
the military base in Indianapolis. With his dependency on
his thick glasses, he was told he couldn't be a rifleman and
would be on limited service, not to be sent overseas. But
Lawrence quickly learned how unpredictable war can be.
After finishing training as a medic, he was shipped to
North Africa as part of a replacement force. After a brief
stay in Oran, Algeria, Lawrence found himself in Italy
during the summer of 1944, ready to immediately replace
any man who fell casualty to enemy fire. With the
successful Allied breakout from Normandy, the Allies
decided it was time to deliver a knockout blow to the
reeling Germans. On August 15, 1944, the Allies landed in
southern France, smashing the thin German defenses as
they raced north to link up with troops from Normandy.
Shortly after the beginning of Dragoon, the group of
replacements, including Lawrence, received orders to head
for the front. Lawrence and Eric Essenwein, a man he
had befriended since his draft, packed their gear in two
bags as they prepared to leave their barracks. At the train
station they joined a line of nervous but eager men

boarding the train that would take them to their assigned units. The line slowly worked its way into railroad cars, until it was Eric's turn to board. As Lawrence stepped from the platform to follow him, the sergeant loading the men said they were full and Lawrence would not be going to the front, at least not right now. This came as a huge inconvenience, because not only was Lawrence separated from his friend, but Eric also had half his gear, and Lawrence had half of his. Sadly, the two comrades were forced to part ways, with Lawrence returning to his barracks and Eric heading off to join the Third Infantry Division. Five days later, a joyful Lawrence Bott again left his barracks. This time he was actually being assigned to a unit, which just happened to be the Third Infantry Division! Excited to rejoin his friend, Lawrence wasted no time after his arrival to find the mail clerk who could tell him which unit Eric had been assigned to. What the clerk told him came as a huge shock, Eric Essenwein had been killed shortly after arriving at the front while attempting to help a wounded comrade, and Lawrence was his friend's replacement. Devastated by the loss of his friend, Lawrence had to force himself back into focus. There was still a war to be won, and as a medic, it was his responsibility to care for the wounded.

In the coming months, Lawrence fought in many brutal and chaotic battles across southern France, as the Allies drove the Germans back towards the Fatherland. Assigned to the squad of Sergeant Russell Dunham, who would receive the Medal of Honor for his actions during the Battle of the Bulge, Lawrence would be known throughout the unit as "Doc"

Though he got to know many of the men in his unit, Lawrence was reluctant to forge any friendships like he had with Eric Essenwein. He simply couldn't bear becoming friends with a man only to lose him to enemy fire. This fear was proven a true possibility on October 28, 1944, near the town of Saint Die. The day started out like any other. Lawrence woke up in a foxhole and had a cup of coffee with the man he shared the foxhole with. This day it happened to be Sergeant Jack Palman, a man from Texas who, with the traditional draw, began the morning with his usual saying, "You know Doc, there ain't nothing better than a cup of coffee and a cigarette in the morning." After breakfast the unit began to advance west to link up with two friendly battalions that had been cut off by the Germans. They quickly ran into heavy enemy resistance, and the Americans were pinned down. The company commander was injured and passed command to his lieutenant, who almost immediately after took a bullet to the neck. Lawrence had been standing right next to the lieutenant when he was hit and immediately realized the man's jugular vein had been cut. As he tried desperately to stop the bleeding, Lawrence yelled to Sergeant Dunham, informing him he was now in command. Lawrence lost count of the number of injuries he treated that day as he rushed around the battlefield, with men crying "Medic!" everywhere. Had it not been for Sergeant Lucian Adams, who rushed and took out the machinegun nests pinning the company down, Lawrence doubted any of them would have survived that day. Many men did not survive, including Jack Palmer, the man Lawrence had shared breakfast with just a few hours earlier.

As the Americans established a base closer St. Die, they continued to face stubborn enemy resistance. At night, they came under a heavy German artillery barrage. One lucky shot hit the unit's ammo dump and immediately the familiar call, "Medic!" broke out.

Crawling out of his bunker, Lawrence used the light from the artillery explosions to find the man calling for help. He quickly dragged him back to the bunker. As he applied first aid, the wounded soldier would not stop thanking Lawrence for saving his life, promising to get him a medal for his actions. "Forget the medal," Lawrence replied "Just get me the hell out of here!"

On Thanksgiving in 1944, as the Americans cleared the remnants of German resistance in a small village, Lawrence spotted through the thick rain a German soldier escaping to a camouflaged car. Because he was a medic, Lawrence was forbidden by the Geneva Convention from carrying a weapon. But he wasn't going to let this stop him from preventing the German's escape. Stuffing his hand in the pocket of his raincoat, he shouted, "Hands up!" pointing his coat like he had a gun. The gamble worked, and the German soldier surrendered. Lawrence quickly called for backup and his friends, who were allowed to carry guns, took the German (who they believed to be the chauffeur of the colonel commanding forces in the town) into custody.

In the violence of war, Lawrence didn't just take care of his fellow Americans. When civilians were caught in the crossfire, he was there to help. One day, as his unit set up an observation post in a farmhouse, a Frenchman approached the American position and said his mother had been badly injured in an American air attack. Knowing German forces were still in the area, Lawrence grabbed an old black dress and other various pieces of clothing and followed the man to his house, disguised as a local peasant. After arriving, he examined the woman's wound. She had taken shrapnel to the thigh, but the injury had become infected. Knowing he could do very little with his personal medical supplies, Lawrence immediately radioed for an ambulance.

Arriving in Kaysersberg as the cold winter weather set in, Lawrence's unit managed to seize half the town, but the remaining German defenders refused to be dislodged. As he hurried from one position to another, Lawrence heard the crack of a sniper rifle as a bullet hit the ground inches from him. Breaking into a full-out sprint, he quickly made it to safety without another shot being fired. The sniper clearly had no idea how fast Lawrence could run when scared!

The fight for Kaysersberg only intensified when the German offensive in the Ardennes began. A week into the Battle of the Bulge, Lawrence came down with tonsillitis and was pulled from his unit. After spending two weeks in the hospital, the medical officer told Lawrence he was better and asked if he was ready to go back to the front. "Sir, I am a soldier who follows orders," Lawrence said, "but I'm not volunteering for anything." "In that case, you're going to the front. That's an order!" the officer replied.

It was during his time in the hospital that Lawrence's sergeant, Russell Dunham, performed the action that earned him the Medal of Honor. On January 8, 1945, with his unit pinned down and in danger of being wiped out, Sergeant Dunham took out three German machinegun nests, or, as Lawrence later put it, "tried to win the war single handedly." Though he had never been eager to be in the middle of the action, Lawrence still wishes he had been there that day.

No sooner had Lawrence returned to the front, than he was again removed from the action-only this time, taken behind German lines. On the night if January 23, while trying to seize a bridge over the Ill River, Lawrence and his unit were scattered by heavy enemy fire. While he and about a dozen others sought cover in a nearby barn, the Germans surrounded them, and a Tiger tank blocked the only door. Out of options, Lawrence and the others surrendered. Their German captors lined the Americans up beside the road for what seemed like hours. Finally, they were told they were going to be killed because the German forces in the area were under intense pressure from the Allies and no men could be spared to watch the prisoners. Death seemed almost appealing to the exhausted, freezing, starving Lawrence Bott. After shaking hands and saying goodbye to each other, the Americans waited quietly for the end to come.

The end never came. For some unknown reason, the Germans decided not to shoot their prisoners and instead began to march them back to Germany. During his time as a Prisoner of War, Lawrence was liberated, recaptured, and then escaped, only to be captured again! He was liberated for good on April 29, 1945.

Lawrence was promoted to corporal after being liberated from the German prison. Although he had lost 80 pounds in four months and was very undernourished and weak, Lawrence was alive and was extremely grateful for his survival, knowing many had perished in the German prisons. One can only imagine the relief his family had when they were informed that he was alive after having been declared Missing in Action for over four months.

In June of 1945, Lawrence and other former POWs boarded a ship for home. On the voyage across the Atlantic, the starved former prisoners were slowly nursed back to health by being given a certain portion of food each day. They were not allowed to have any more than what was given to them. To avoid any trouble, armed guards were placed outside the ship's kitchen.

After settling back down in the United States, Lawrence attended Columbus University, planning to be a dentist, but changed his mind when he realized how complicated the political situation would be to get him into dental school. He then changed courses and after graduation became a salesman working for several different companies. He married his wife, Lois, on November 4, 1950, and they had four sons together.

Today Lawrence and his wife live as a retired couple in Columbus. They enjoy the company of their friends and family, now including 11 grandchildren. Lawrence, realizing that future generations wanted to hear the stories of those who fought in World War II, has written a book called "Memories of an Infantry Combat Medic in World War 2." This is his story told firsthand and has been put into the Library of Congress.

Though it has been many years since the end of World War II, people have not forgotten the bravery and heroism of men like Lawrence Bott. In November of 2010, Lawrence and a select group of veterans gathered in the rotunda of the Ohio State Capital to be knighted by the nation of France and Ohio Governor Ted Strickland as Knights of the Legion of Honor. The man known as Doc has now achieved a new title, Sir Lawrence Bott.

He wonders to this day how he made it out alive, because he had brushed the wings of death more than once in his time overseas. Lawrence is not saddened by his service, but would not want to go through it again, and hopes that future generations won't have to.

The "Soft Underbelly" of Europe

WITH AMERICA AND JAPAN NOW at war, Germany and Italy immediately declared their allegiance to Japan. War now encompassed ever corner of the globe. As young American men created mile-long lines outside recruitment offices, battles continued to rage from the snow of west Russia, to the sweltering heat of Guadalcanal, to the blistering dry African desert.

Though the United States was now at war, the nation as a whole was unprepared for actually fighting. The American army was small, and not equipped for such a large conflict. Although thousands of volunteers were rushing to enlist, these men would take time to train for battle. Despite being the most powerful industrial nation on the planet, it would take time and resources for the United States to fully have enough weapons of war to begin to fight back. In the meantime, the British would have to hold their own.

During most of 1942 the United States was unable to contribute to the fight against Hitler. Although the Soviets had thrown the Germans back from Moscow, they soon found themselves in retreat in the south, as the Hitler's armies made a new push to seize the vast oil fields in the Caucuses. Though Britain had survived the Luftwaffe's blitz, its forces in Egypt threatened to be overrun with the arrival of German Field Marshal Erwin Rommel. One of the most skilled commanders of the Second World War, Rommel, nicknamed the Desert Fox, proved a master at the German blitzkrieg, or lighting war. Under his leadership, the German and Italian forces drove the British deep into Egypt, and soon the Suez Canal was within the Axis grasp. Hitler had reached the peak of his power. His armies held an iron fist over all of Europe, their reach stretching from the Atlantic to the Volga, and from the Arctic mountains of Norway to the Egyptian desert. To many, taking on such a powerful military state might have seemed impossible. But the war was far from over, and in time the Allies, with skill and determination, combined with several major failures on the part of the Germans, would bring about the halting and then reversal of the Nazi gains.

By the fall of 1942, Hitler had become too absorbed with the Eastern Front, as the titanic armies of Germany and the Soviet Union fought a vicious battle for the city of Stalingrad, to hear Rommel's pleas for more supplies to be sent to his Africa Corps. With his forces already stretched to their limits and most of their supply ships being sunk in the Mediterranean by Allied Naval and Air Forces, Rommel's forces were becoming weaker as they gained ground. The British, under the command of General Bernard Montgomery, meanwhile were able to concentrate their forces in a line just west of the town of El Alamein, and by October the Germans had lost momentum.

A stalemate now seemed to begin, but it would be short lived. The British now had the upper hand over the exhausted and thinly stretched Germans. Their superior strength gave the British the ability to launch a new attack that began on October 23, 1942. Despite outnumbering the Germans two to one, the Allied advance proved meticulously slow at first due to tenacious resistance from the Germans, who had built a strong defensive line along the entire front. Minefields, nicknamed "The Devil's Garden," were the main obstacle that kept the British at bay. Demolition teams had to clear a path through the fields for the tanks and infantry that were to carry out the attack. As if defusing land mines isn't dangerous enough, they had to do it under constant machine gun and artillery fire. For over a week, the two sides fought a brutal battle of attrition, with the British slowly gaining ground at the cost of heavy casualties on both sides. But the British were a stronger force, and the RAF had complete control of the skies, flying hundreds of sorties a day that crippled German defenses. By November 2, it was clear the Germans had lost the battle, and their only chance of survival was to retreat. Rommel sent a telegram to Hitler requesting permission to fall back. The Fuhrer responded by ordering him to hold his position and not to yield a yard of ground whatever the cost. Though not wanting to be one of the few to disobey Hitler, Rommel realized staying would be suicidal, and against his orders Rommel instructed his men to retreat. As the Axis forces in Africa fell into chaos, their situation was made even made more dire on November 8, when a joint American-British force, lead by American General Dwight Eisenhower, landed in the French colonies of Morocco and Algeria. Code named Operation Torch, the Allied invasion was the Americans' baptism of fire. Though the French troops stationed in Africa now reported to the Vichy French Government, a puppet state set up by the Germans, the Allied leaders still hoped they would not resist the invasion. In some places their hopes came true, with French soldiers laying down their weapons as the Allies approached. But in other places, green American troops came under fire as they landed on the beaches. After fighting through the coastal defenses, the Allies quickly pressed inland, and any remaining French resistance collapsed.

Rommel's troops now found themselves trapped in Tunisia, with Montgomery's army to the east and Eisenhower's to the west. By this time, neither side had the strength to launch an attack. The winter passed in relative quiet while fresh supply reinforcements were brought to the front.

The violence returned full force on February 14, 1943, when German units, finally having been sufficiently reinforced and resupplied, attacked the city of Sidi Bou Zid, a major Allied communications center. The hardened German veterans easily overpowered the inexperienced American soldiers, who had seen little or no action in Operation Touch. On February 19, the Germans followed up with an attack through Kasserine Pass, with the objective of seizing supply dumps just behind the Allied front. The attack, led by Rommel himself, made swift initial progress, overrunning the disorganized and untested American defenders. The Allies were thrown into chaos and scrambled to fill the gap Rommel had made in their lines. In three days the Germans had advanced fifty miles, and, feeling they had significantly crippled the American forces and achieved the rest of their objectives, began to withdraw east.

The Germans would launch two additional offensives in the coming weeks, one aimed at pushing back the British army in Libya, and the other to retake Northern Tunisia from Eisenhower's forces. Both were repelled with heavy losses, and the Germans failed to achieve another victory like the one at Kasserine Pass. Rommel now realized that victory in Africa was no longer possible and told Hitler their best chance was to evacuate the troops. Hitler refused, ordering that Tunisia be held, and any chance of the survival of the Axis units in Africa vanished. On April 22, the Allies launched their own offensive, with Montgomery's army attacking from the south and east, and Eisenhower's troops from the west. The Germans were driven steadily north toward the beaches of the Mediterranean. On May 13, the 240,00 Axis soldiers in North Africa surrendered. This, coupled with the defeat of the German 6th Army at Stalingrad earlier in the year, dealt massive blows to Hitler's armies, and was the beginning of the end for the Third Reich.

With victory in North Africa, debate now filled Allied Headquarters everywhere. As to what the next move should be. Joseph Stalin argued for an invasion of France as soon as possible to take the pressure off the Soviets, who were still in a desperate position despite their victory at Stalingrad. Plans were already being drawn up for a possible landing in France in August of 1943. The British, chiefly Prime Minister Churchill, advocated for a Mediterranean-based strategy. They argued that German submarines in the Atlantic were still too much of a threat for potential landing to be feasible. The British high command also pointed out the American military was still not strong or experienced enough for such a massive undertaking and that there were not enough landing craft to transport the necessary number of troops. The debate continues to this day as to whether the Allies could have launched a successful invasion of France in 1943. While we will never know for certain whether it could have been done, what we do know is the Americans reluctantly consented to the British urging to attack the "soft underbelly of Europe" by attacking Sicily and using the island as a base to attack Italy, home of Hitler's number one ally, Benito Mussolini.

On July 10, Operation Husky, the Allied invasion of Sicily began with simultaneous landings by British and American airborne divisions behind enemy lines. The

paratroopers' mission was to hold off enemy
reinforcements heading for the targeted beaches until the
amphibious troops could get a foothold on the island.
This first major Allied paratroop drop of the war nearly
met with disaster. Bad weather and strong winds scattered
the airborne units across a wide area. The nervous crews
of Allied ships fired on the transport planes as they passed
overhead, and a large number of casualties that night were
the result of friendly fire incidents. Though the airborne
landings did not go at all smoothly, the disorganization
actually helped the Allies, as reports of paratroopers being
spotted everywhere poured into Axis headquarters. As the
paratroopers gathered what friends they could find and
began to move toward their objectives, with multiple
locations under attack, sowing chaos and confusion
among the Axis high command.

The amphibious landings did not suffer any similar
setbacks and encountered surprisingly light resistance on
the beaches. By the end of the first day, the Allies held a
beachhead stretching over 100 miles along the south and
east coasts of Sicily. The victory temporarily seemed
threatened as the joint German and Italian forces
counterattacked with their main force, which had been
stationed inland as a reserve. But with reinforcements
pouring onto the beaches, and support from the guns of
large naval ships, the Allies beat back the Axis attack.

With the Allied position in Sicily now impossible to
remove, German General Albert Kesselring ordered his
troops to abandon the west flank to concentrate their
forces in the northeastern corner of the island. The British
and Americans were quick to seize the territory the Axis
had abandoned, capturing the island capital of Palermo on
July 22. But the speed of their advance slowed as they
reached the dug-in Axis units in the Northeast. To

General Kesselring, no doubt remained that Sicily was a lost cause, and a gradual withdrawal to the Italian mainland had already begun. In just seventeen days, 135,000 German and Italian troops were evacuated to Italy. Heavy antiaircraft frustrated Allied aircraft attempts to stop the transfer of men and equipment. On August 17, the last Axis troops left the island, and Sicily fell completely under Allied control.

With control of Sicily came complete Allied domination of the Mediterranean Sea, dealing a deathblow to Italian morale, while giving American soldiers and sailors vital combat experience. The situation was made even better by the fall of Hitler's closest ally and role model, Benito Mussolini. The people of Italy had never held the Duce's passion for a second Roman Empire and from the beginning lacked any real enthusiasm for the war. After the catastrophe in Africa and with the Allies now at their country's doorstep, the Italian Grand Council deposed Mussolini on the 24th of July.

The new government immediately began secret negotiations to surrender to the Allies, agreeing not only to end all fighting against the Allies, but to allow occupation of the country and to join the fight against Germany. A window of opportunity now appeared before General Eisenhower and his commanders. If they could land troops unopposed in Italy and seize control of the peninsula, their armies would be able to threaten Germany from the south, making an invasion of Western Europe less urgent or completely unnecessary. Churchill's claim that this was the "soft underbelly" of Europe seemed right.

On September 3, 1943, Italy secretly signed the Armistice, and British troops from Sicily began landing on the mainland the same day. As hoped, they landed virtually unopposed and began to advance up the "toe" of the peninsula. But the bright hopes at the onset of the invasion would soon be dashed. Hitler, anticipating Italy's surrender, sent reinforcements into the country, under the guise of assisting in the defense of an ally's homeland. In reality the troops were there to dismantle the Italian military as soon as the Allied invasion began. Though the initial landing would be quick and peaceful, as the Allies began to advance inland, the Germans were waiting for them.

On September 9, the main invasion of Italy began with the American Fifth Army landing near the town of Salerno. It immediately became apparent that the troops were in for a tough fight. As the landing craft approached the beaches, a loudspeaker on shore proclaimed "Come in and give up. We have you covered." Undaunted, the Americans hit the beach. They immediately came under heavy fire, and the entire invasion force struggled to advance. The Germans quickly brought reinforcements to the landing site and their counterattack began on September 13, almost overrunning the American beachhead. The American troops were saved only by overwhelming air support and naval bombardments of German positions. With the arrival of the British troops that had landed farther south, the Germans lost the advantage and withdrew north, with the Allies in hot pursuit. Though vigorous in their march up the "boot" of Italy, the Allies quickly found that the terrain heavily favored the defenders. The uneven, rocky ground, open valleys, and large mountains gave the Germans natural defensive positions. The advance remained at a slow but steady speed as the Germans fought a delaying action to prepare for their main line of defense.

The Gustav line was a series of defensive networks, designed by Field Marshal Albert Kesselring, stretching across the entire peninsula about 100 miles south of Rome. The Allies reached the German positions there in November, and the advance stopped in the face of fierce resistance.

Attack after attack was launched, but to no avail. Unable to break through the Gustav line, the Allies resorted to an alternative strategy: another amphibious assault north of the German positions, to cut them off and attack from behind. Called Operation Shingle, American and British forces landed at the town of Anzio on January 22, 1944. The Germans were not expecting the attack and not a single soldier was there to oppose the landing. On the first day the troops would penetrate three miles inland and capture the port of Anzio.

Though the success of the operation depended on a speedy attack on the undefended German rear before they had time to react, General John Lucas, commander of the Allied landing force, hesitated. Lacking confidence in the plan and thinking he lacked the necessary resources for such a swift strike, Lucas decided to build up the defenses on the beachhead before advancing. It would prove to be a tragic mistake. As soon as word reached the German commanders about the landings, Field Marshal Kesselring sent every man he could spare to Anzio. Within a day, the Germans seized the high ridges and hills surrounding the beach, and the Allies lost the initiative.

For the next four months the battle of Anzio would rage, with the Allied troops holding a precarious position on that tiny beachhead. The troops were always at risk of being driven back into the sea, and were unable to be relieved by the friendly forces to the south, still held up at the Gustav line. The fight for Italy became a war of attrition, each side slowly chipping away at the other's strength, and only the strongest would be the victor. Gradually the pressure the Allies exerted on the Germans proved too much, and by late May the Gustav line finally began to crumble. With the German defenses cracking, the Allied forces, bottled up at Anzio, managed to break out. At this point the Allied objective of cutting off the main enemy units could still be accomplished. Most of the retreating Germans were still south of Anzio and could have been trapped between the troops there and the forces advancing from the north. But General Truscott, who had replaced Lucas, received orders to turn his forces north and reach Rome as soon as possible. This gave the Germans the opening they needed to escape, and live to fight another day. On June 4, 1944, American troops entered Rome. Kesselring had declared the capital an open city and the only people blocking the Americans were the crowds of Italian citizens rushing to great their liberators. The liberation of Rome was a huge victory and boost to morale throughout the Allied ranks, and it came on the eve of another climactic battle, farther north in France, at a place called Normandy.

Alton Litsinberger
October 9, 1925 – February 17, 2012

Alton Litsinberger was born on October 9, 1925, in Delaware, Ohio, where he spent most of his childhood. While growing up, he loved riding bikes on a summer's day.

On September 23, 1943, Alton and his dad took a long drive to Lockbourne Army Base in Columbus to take his physical examination. He passed every test except the eye exam; because of his bad eye, he couldn't join the Aviation Cadet Training. On the way home, Alton decided to enlist in the Army before he was drafted, since all the boys drafted were sent to the Navy, and he wasn't a good swimmer.

On October 14, 1943, Alton received orders to report for active duty. Fifteen days later he took a time-consuming train ride to Fort Thomas, Kentucky, just across the Ohio River from Cincinnati. At Fort Thomas, Alton and other recruits took another physical exam and were issued official army uniforms along with other military equipment. After two weeks at Fort Thomas, Alton boarded a long train ride to the Army Field Artillery School, known as Fort Sill, in Oklahoma.

Besides the strenuous military training, there where duties the men were assigned to during boot camp. Kitchen Police, or KP for short, required waking up at 0400 hours to help the cooks prepare a healthy breakfast for 100 men, and then serve them. After each meal, they would help clean the dirty mess hall and kitchen. Alton's main jobs were to peel fresh potatoes and wash used dishes. The upside to KP was that they got to eat as much as their stomachs desired. Guard duty required guarding different areas around camp. The soldiers spent two hours on duty and four off throughout the night. The worst was latrine duty; men had to clean used sinks, and showers. Fire duty meant keeping the furnace going and making sure no fires broke out.

After he finished the Enlisted Communication course on June 17, 1944, Alton transferred to a holding area, waiting for an assignment to a permanent unit. Like other excited soldiers there, Alton spent his time as an Officer's Aid. This basically meant cleaning their quarters, shining their shoes, and being their errand boys.

Alton left on the last day of June and was assigned to the 257th Field Artillery Battalion Headquarters Battery. Before joining this unit he had a seven-day pass to spend at home, and he decided to use it. After his week at home, Alton bid another sad good-bye to his friends and family and boarded a train to Camp Gordon, Georgia, where the 257th was stationed. He arrived on July 10, 1944. Over the next two long months, the men of the 257th were put through tough combat training. They took vigorous hikes between 5 to 25 miles long; they were trained to fire big machine guns and huge bazookas; and became good marksmen. Alton was made both a truck driver and fifty-caliber machine gunner.

On September 13, the unit left Camp Gordon for Camp Shanks, New York, where they arrived the next day. The first thing they had to do after arrival was remove any identification of what unit they were assigned to. This helped ensure that enemy spies wouldn't know what outfits were going overseas. Alton overlooked a single patch on his uniform and was restricted to camp for several days as punishment.

While at Camp Shanks the men were trained on how to get off a ship quickly if it was torpedoed and how to climb down a cargo net into a boat. If they had a pass, the men could spend their free time in New York City, where nothing ever closed and no one ever sleeps.

After almost two long weeks at Camp Shanks, Alton joined several thousand men aboard a British ship, the Uruguay, boat number NY-396. They left New York very late under the cover of darkness on the night of September 29. The Uruguay joined several other ships and formed a fierce convoy. The trip across the Atlantic was no luxury cruise. Many men got seasick, and the food, mainly just ham, cabbage and some kind of bread, wasn't very appetizing. A couple of days into the trip, Alton decided to live off the few candy bars he had brought with him. To prevent being spotted by German submarines, no lights could be on at night. This made it almost impossible to go out on deck or read a single book; the men could only lie in their hammocks. Sometimes for fun they played poker or shot dice.

A week into the trip the Uruguay developed engine trouble. The ship had to stop, and the rest of the convoy continued to England. Two small Canadian Navy ships, called Corvettes, stayed with the Uruguay to defend it. On the second day they were stranded, the Corvettes started dropping their depth charges. Alton and the other men aboard the Uruguay put on their life jackets and crowded on the top deck where they would be safer and ready to evacuate if the ship was torpedoed. Fortunately, no torpedo ever came, and, with the engines repaired, the Uruguay continued its route to Bristol, England. They finally docked on October 9th--Alton's 19th birthday!

Once in England, Alton and fellow soldiers were deployed to a town called Wimborne Minister and put in civilian houses. Alton's machine gun section had the second floor of a nice British family's house. The family was very nice and even fed them wonderful meals. In return for their kindness the soldiers used the outside stairs so as not to bother the family.

The troops continued strenuous training and had new guns that worked really well. In their free time, the men traveled the beautiful countryside to see the sights and other towns like Pool and Bournemouth. Alton and his friend, Nick, even went to London on a weekend pass and saw firsthand the horrible destruction the German bombers and buzz bombs had caused. More than once Alton and other soldiers were forced to find cover in bomb shelters to escape the German attacks. Alton and Nick loved to visit a British air base on Sundays and catch a ride on the bombers the pilots were taking up on training exercises. One Sunday they arrived just as a squadron of aircraft were taking off and scrambled to catch the last bomber before it took off. Alton's favorite place to ride was with the tail gunner, all the way at the back of the plane next to a big machine gun. On this particular Sunday, as he made his way to his favorite perch, he passed through the bomb bay and saw it was filled with bombs. "This is strange," he thought to himself, "they don't usually put bombs on the plane for training exercises, they only load bombs when they are on... combat missions." Yes, that's right, on that Sunday, Alton and Nick bombed Europe. Although he had a bright future ahead of him as a member of a bomber crew, Alton "retired" after his first mission. He and Nick never flew on one of those planes again. But they did get to brag that they were the first in their outfit to see combat.

When the Battle of the Bulge began on December 16th, 1944, the 257th was ordered to the Ardennes. They left England aboard LSTs (Landing Ship Tanks) on the 21st of December and arrived in France the next day. The LSTs let the trucks disembark some ways offshore to avoid getting beached. Alton's truck was the first to disembark and ended up in four feet of water. The engine had a tough, waterproof coating so it could still work, but Alton didn't have waterproof clothing and got wet on the way to shore.

Alton arrived in the combat area on Christmas Eve 1944 when they joined General Patton's Third Army. The unit was assigned to several different Field Artillery Groups. They began firing the big 155 Howitzers to support frontline soldiers. The men soon found the cruel Germans were not the only enemy in the Ardennes. The weather proved to be another difficulty. The temperature would often go below zero, and snow was everywhere. The men lived in foxholes or wet bunkers dug out of the ground and covered with logs and dirt. If they were lucky, they might find a destroyed, bombed-out house to sleep in.

Despite the rugged terrain, fierce weather, and a determined German army, the Allies pushed on. Alton participated in the attack to relieve the beleaguered Americans in Bastogne. The unit then moved to southern Luxembourg and then Germany, where they remained till the Battle of the Bulge ended on January 25, 1945.

In early April, Alton and the unit were sent back across France to the area around the town of Royan. The Germans at Royan had been bypassed when the Allies took France and the town had to be taken. The men of the 257th fired nearly 6,000 rounds at the town and destroyed it. On April 23 Alton received his first promotion to Private First Class. Shortly after that, the battalion was ordered back to Germany. But the war ended before they got to the front.

On May 15 the men of the 257th took up positions at the German town of Nordlingen. They were ordered to patrol the area for Germans who didn't want to give up the fight. The battalion was demobilized on October 6, 1945, and the men were sent to many different outfits and prepared to head back to the United States. Alton boarded a train to Bremerhaven, Germany; there, they would board a ship to sail back to the States. On the way to Bremerhaven, the railcar carrying their gear caught fire and burned everything. Alton unfortunately lost two tailor-made uniforms and all the great pictures he had taken and not sent home to his family.

Alton arrived back home in March 1946 and quickly set out to find some milk to drink.

Over the next few months, he began searching for a job and found one as a truck mechanic. In April 1950 Alton married Virginia and they had two kids, Lou Ann and Tracy, and three grandkids, Jena, Ashley, and Michael.

Alton's service is acknowledged by the medals he received--the Good Conduct medal, the Victory medal, Battle of the Bulge medal, and E.A.M.E (European, African, Middle Eastern) theater ribbon with four Bronze Stars.

The one thing that saddens Alton is that he did not remain in the Army, a decision he regrets. When asked what he would like future generations to remember about the Battle of the Bulge, he wants everyone to remember the horrible cold weather during the course of the Battle and that WE WON.

Dante Toneguzzo
November 11, 1922 -

Born on Veterans Day, 1922 Dante Toneguzzo was born and raised in Columbus Ohio. Growing up, he was lucky to live in a house just down the street from Tifman's Field, an important place at the time because it was the only location in Columbus big enough to host a circus. Whenever a circus group came to town, they would always pass right by Dante's house on their way to Tifman's field. As a little boy, Dante would hang on the screen door so he could peer out the window to watch the performers, clowns, elephants go by. He developed a love for the circus that still persists eighty-five years later. Another thing he learned to love during his childhood, was the feeling of being a team player and working alongside others, which he developed during from his years as a captain of a football team. This would help him appreciate the camaraderie of the Army life all the more.

In December of 1943, with World War II raging, Dante Toneguzzo decided to enlist in the Coast Guard. The only thing stopping him was President Roosevelt's temporary ban on naval enlistments, the purpose being to drive people into the Army where they were urgently needed for the planned Normandy invasion. Despite this, he still went to the Coast Guard recruitment office to sign up and take his physical test. The recruiter told him they would be ordered to basic training as soon as the enlistment ban was lifted. A few days later, Mr. Toneguzzo did receive a letter, but it wasn't from the Coast Guard, it was the Army. He had been drafted, and was to report for duty at Fort Thomas, Kentucky. With the enlistment ban still in place, Mr. Toneguzzo had no choice but to go. Upon arrival, he received his first assignment, laundry duty. Though he protested the assignment should go to some of the older recruits, who were in their thirties and had families, and that a young man like him should have a more combat related role, the officer did not change his mind. So it was, that while washing clothes at Fort Thomas, Mr. Toneguzzo received, too late, a letter that said "You have been accepted into the Coast Guard."

Sick of laundry duty, Mr. Toneguzzo finally got out of it by volunteering to become a paratrooper. After completing his airborne training at Fort Bragg, North Carolina, he was assigned to the 507th airborne regiment. During his time with the airborne, his last name was shortened and he became known as just Guzzo.

Shortly after being deployed to England, came an unforgettable day in Mr. Guzzo's life. The entire unit was gathered in a large hanger, there, laid out for all to see, was a map of Normandy, France. The men were told that Operation Overlord, the Allied invasion of Nazi held France was about to begin. The operation called for three American airborne regiments to land behind enemy lines and prevent German supplies and reinforcements from disrupting the Allied landings on the beaches. Because the 504th airborne regiment was still under strength from casualties it had suffered in the invasion of Sicily. Private Guzzo and the 507th were to take their place and become part of the 82nd airborne division.

In the late hours of June 5, 1944 Private Guzzo, climbed aboard a C-47 and ascended into the sky to join the thousands of planes, flying almost wingtip to wingtip in a formation that stretched over eight miles long. All carrying the airborne divisions to their drop zones in Normandy. As soon as the American aircraft entered Nazi airspace, enemy anti aircraft guns opened fire. Terrified of the flak that seemed to be coming from everywhere, the pilot of Mr. Guzzo's aircraft decided to have the paratroopers jump even though they weren't over the drop zone. Jumping out of the air plane, Mr. Guzzo floated down to earth as the sky around him continued to explode with enemy flak. He could only watch helplessly as a nearby American plane burst into a ball of fire, and joined him in his decent. After landing Mr. Guzzo quickly realized he was nowhere near where he was supposed to be. Turning to the man that had landed beside him, he was mortified to see the paratrooper had lost an arm and a leg. Knowing there was nothing he could do, but hope a medic found the man in time, Mr. Guzzo began to grope his way through the unfamiliar, pitch dark, German infested territory. Relying purely on instinct and luck he managed to find a handful of fellow paratroopers, and over the next few days, their group gradually grew in size.

The terrain in Normandy was difficult and dangerous, especially the hedgerows that were everywhere. Too tall to see over and too thick to remove, the enemy could be right on the other side of the overgrown hedges and they would never know. Directly behind the point man for his unit, Mr. Guzzo and the others stopped when he found a small hole in the hedgerow alongside them. As the point man peered through the hole, he almost immediately fell backward as an enemy sniper on the other side shot him in the head. Shocked and shaken, Mr. Guzzo and the others avoided the holes in hedgerows from then on. Despite their caution, on June 11, after five days of constant fighting, Mr. Guzzo was injured when a piece of shrapnel struck his leg. Not wanting to leave his comrades while there was still a war to fight, he ignored the medics urging that he be evacuated, and stayed on the frontline until all the paratroopers were withdrawn.

By the summer of 1944, the 504th airborne regiment had regained its full strength. With more airborne regiments than needed, the 82nd Division commander had to let one go. He choose to remove the highly disliked 507th, infamously known as the "Bastard Outfit". Now a regiment without a division, the men of the 507th were disregarded. As Mr. Guzzo said "We were now nobodies. We were somebody in Normandy, now we were nobody."

For a while, the 507th had no assignments, until the arrival of the 17th airborne division in late August. The decision was made to attach the 507th to the 17th, and all the men were issued the division's patch, the Eagle claw. In comparing their patch with the patch of the Eagle head that the 101st received, Mr. Guzzo and the others would complain "They get the Eagle's head while we get the chicken's ass."

Excited for a new assignment on advance duty, Mr. Guzzo traveled with a group of men with the same assignment. When they arrived a captain was there to inform them of their new assignment. They would now be orderlies for glider pilots. Knowing the dangers and losses the glider crews had suffered in Normandy, Mr. Guzzo was not at all interested in flying in one, so he spoke up "Captain, you can't order me to join a glider crew." "Of course I can," the officer said "I am a Captain." "No you can't," Mr. Guzzo argued "I have to volunteer for that kind of job." Angered that his orders were being challenged, the Captain responded firmly "Private, you WILL be a orderly for a glider crew." Having lost the argument, Mr. Guzzo did the only other thing he could do, at the first opportunity; he grabbed his things and took the day long train ride back to his old base. Though his effort got him out of serving on a glider crew, he was marked as having gone AWOL (Absent With Out Leave) for one day.

Reassigned to a service company, Mr. Guzzo now felt he had it made. Being nowhere near the frontline, he had few duties and got three square meals a day. His relaxing job ended quite suddenly however, when the German's launched their Ardennes offensive and the Battle of the Bulge began. With the reinforcements desperately needed, Mr. Guzzo was put in a replacement outfit and sent back to the European Continent. There he got the worst job an infantry man could have... carrying bazooka ammo. Carrying 10 rockets in a sling over his shoulder, five in across the front, five on his back, he was basically a walking explosion waiting to happen. "Whenever you encountered a tank, you could only hope he (the guy firing the bazooka) hit it on the first shot. Cause if he doesn't, the tank will fire back, and it will get you." Mr. Guzzo recalled. When the German offensive was finally beaten back after weeks of bitter fighting, Mr. Guzzo was able to drop the bazooka ammo and join C Company. But serving in the replacement company proved a good thing as it taught Mr. Guzzo a lesson he carried through his military service and the rest of his life. "When you get a replacement, treat him like one of you." Mr. Guzzo says "He might be the one to save your life. I always taught that to all my troops."

Following the German defeat in the Battle of the Bulge, the Allies resumed their offensive into the enemy's homeland. Mr. Guzzo was amongst those who pushed forward, across the Rhine River and into the heart of

Hitler's Reich. On April 9, 1945, Mr. Guzzo's and his squad were stopped in their tracks and pinned down when they encountered two enemy pill boxes. With enemy machine guns firing everywhere, it seemed impossible to move without getting shot. As he lay there, wondering what to do next, Mr. Guzzo suddenly heard a voice "Go get em, Guzzo. You can do it." The voice seemed to be coming from the sky, but looking up and all around, he couldn't see anybody talking to him. A little confused but greatly inspired, Mr. Guzzo picked himself and ran towards the first pillbox, zigzagging back and forth to avoid the machine gunners lethal spray. He should have died a hundred times during that run, but somehow made it to the first pillbox unscathed. Throwing a grenade inside, the structure he neutralized the enemy position. He then moved quickly to the second pillbox throwing another grenade inside and eliminating the remaining machine gun. In a blur of action Mr. Guzzo had eliminated two enemy pill boxes, saved his squad, and taken 14 prisoners. For his actions that day, Mr. Guzzo received the Distinguished Service Cross, the highest Army decoration for bravery besides the Medal of Honor.

When asked what ranks he advanced during his service, Mr. Guzzo will tell people he was a Sergeant for one day. By the spring of 1945, Hitler's Reich was collapsing, and because of they had already seen extensive combat, the 507th remained behind the front line. Newly promoted Sergeant Guzzo, was ordered to take his squad to guard a local warehouse. Upon arrival, the squad discovered one door was locked. The civilian owner was reluctant to reveal what lay behind the door, but the soldiers quickly persuaded him to unlock it. Inside, they found it was full of wine and champagne. With plenty to go around, everybody had more drinks than they should have, and planned to take the remainder back to base with them. When the squad's Commanding Officer stopped by to check up on the men, Mr. Guzzo, using all the strength and skill he could muster, managed to stand up, salute, and said "Sergeant Guzzo reporting for duty." Not pleased with what he saw the commanding officer told his drunken Sergeant to come see him in the morning. The next morning, the now sober Mr. Guzzo nervously approached his CO's quarters. After knocking on the door, he heard the officer say "Come in, Sergeant Guzzo." "Yes, sir?" said Mr. Guzzo as he entered the room. The officer continued, "You may leave now, Private Guzzo."

After the Nazi surrender on May 7, 1945 Mr. Guzzo remained in Europe as part of the occupation force for over a year, returning to the states in December of 1946. When the ship arrived in the harbor, the troops were greeted by several USO girls who were giving the troops 'welcome home' gifts. All the troops had to do was tell them what they wanted. For Mr. Guzzo the decision was easy, "The entire time I was in the service all we had was powdered milk. So when one of the ladies came up to me and asked 'What do you want?', I said "I want milk!" Well, Mr. Guzzo got his milk... and drank all 3 quarts of it. That proved to be enough for a lifetime, as to this day, besides the occasional milkshake, he can't stomach anything with milk in it.

Discharged as a Sergeant (though without the equivalent salary, as the Army hadn't completely forgotten the warehouse fiasco) Dante ToneGuzzo returned to civilian life. Just as it takes more than a day to make a civilian a soldier, it takes more than a day to make a soldier a civilian, so the government put Mr. Guzzo in the transition program called 52/20. He would receive $20 dollars a week for fifty-two weeks, or until he got a job.

With no real expenses to worry about, Mr. Guzzo used the money to go get drunk every night. Of all the things he did in his first few months home, the most memorable event for him was the city dance. It was a girls-ask-boys dance, and Mr. Guzzo went with Louise Lorrettia. The two instantly clicked that night, and just a short while later, married on April 24, 1947. Together they raised three kids and were married over 60 years until Lousie's death in 2006. After his military career, Mr. Guzzo founded his concrete contracting company, working several major jobs for Jack Nichols, Children's Palaces, and the local interstate.

Today Mr. Guzzo continues to reside in his birth town, Columbus, Ohio. He has six grandchildren and a newborn great-granddaughter. He is very proud of being able to serve alongside many great buddies, and though he does miss the friends he lost, he feels no real sadness about service. He wants everyone to remember that World War Two was fought for freedom, and all signs show that no one will forget that. Or the sacrifices of men like Dante ToneGuzzo. In 2001, Mr. Guzzo returned to Normandy, France with his family, for the unveiling of the Paratrooper monument. Located where his regiment was *suppose* to have landed on D-Day, the Monument is dedicated to all Allied paratroopers who jumped into hostile territory on that historic day. Inscribed on the Monument are the names of just a few of the decorated airborne men who jumped over the continent that historic night. Mr. Guzzo has the honor in being one of the seven men from the 507th named on the monument that will stand as a reminder of the price of freedom, for generations to come.

The Great Crusade

The room was quiet with the exception of the howling wind and pounding rain that had become the cause of the tense atmosphere inside. All eyes were on the Allied Supreme Commander, American General Dwight Eisenhower, whose tired face expressed the heavy burden of the decision he now confronted. Every man had been given the chance to voice his opinion, half saying "Yes," the rest saying "No." But ultimately the final decision lay with Eisenhower alone. After a few moments of anxious silence he spoke. "All right," he said "let's go."

SINCE THE MOMENT FRANCE HAD fallen to the Germans, there had always been talk in the Allied camp of how, when, and where to launch an invasion to liberate the country. The British lacked the strength to execute an invasion alone, and the idea did not become feasible until the United States entered the war. The Americans, strongly backed by the Soviets, had been strong advocates of an invasion of Western Europe from the beginning. They felt it was the shortest route to the heart of Germany, would decisively win the war, and, as the Soviets in particular argued, the best way to relieve German pressure on the Eastern Front. British Prime Minister Winston Churchill, fearing a repeat of the heavy losses from the First World War, pushed for an invasion of Italy as a way to attack Germany while avoiding a frontal assault on Hitler's Atlantic Wall. He also argued that the American military did not yet have the strength for such an ambitious undertaking. The British argument prevailed for some time, but as progress in Italy proved slow at best, and pressure mounted from Joseph Stalin in the Soviet Union and from President Roosevelt, Churchill reluctantly consented that the invasion of France would be launched in 1944. General Dwight Eisenhower was appointed Supreme Commander of all Allied Forces and tasked with planning and executing the invasion.

Eisenhower's first task was to pick a location along the coast of France to land his army. He and his commanders quickly narrowed their options to two beaches, the Pas de Calais, in northern France, and Normandy, a small peninsula just north of Brittany. The Pas de Calais was the more obvious choice. It was closer to Britain than any other place in Europe, had several large ports the Allies would need to supply their landing forces following the invasion, and would put the Allied armies in the perfect position to launch their own Blitzkrieg into the heart of Germany. Normandy had only one port in the region, Cherbourg; was much farther from the British mainland; and wouldn't give the Allies immediate access to the German homeland. The Pas de Calais was obviously the better choice, and that is why the Allies picked Normandy. Because of the location's disadvantages the Germans wouldn't expect it. Even after the attack, the Germans might hesitate to send reinforcements, fearing the Allies were attempting to distract them from the real landing at the Pas de Calais.

Code named Operation Overlord, Eisenhower and his commanders set the date for the invasion of Normandy for June 5. June 5, 1944, was a day when both low tide and daybreak came together and a night with a full moon for the airborne units that would be dropped behind enemy lines. The planning and organization was on a scale never seen before. Hundreds of thousands of men were organized into units and rigorously trained across Great Britain. Every kind of weapon imaginable, from rifles and machine guns to tanks and artillery, to bombers and fighters, were being manufactured and assembled in astonishing quantities. Two artificial harbors called Mulberries were built. These unprecedented feats in engineering would be towed across the channel and assembled at the landing beaches. They would act as the Allies' supply station until a port on the mainland could be captured. A pipeline would be built under strict secrecy across the bottom of the channel to pump oil to the invasion force once it landed. All these preparations were impossible to keep secret from the Germans, whose spy planes constantly flew overhead, watching every move the Allies made. The Germans knew the invasion of Western Europe was coming, but did not know where or when, and to preserve that uncertainty, the Allies employed one of the greatest deception operations in history.

During the winter of 1943--44, the German intelligence had gleaned enough information from aerial Recon and double agents piece together the reality of the danger they faced. The First United States Army Group, or FUSAG, under the command of the aggressive General Patton, was training in Kent, England, in preparation for an invasion of the Pas de Calais. Reports indicated that the British Fourth Army, training in Scotland, would launch an invasion of Norway. An Allied landing at Normandy might even be executed as a way to draw German units away from the primary invasion. Since the fall of France, Hitler had spoken of building an Atlantic Wall that stretched along the entire coast from Scandinavia to Spain. Now, with his enemy on the verge of one, maybe several, attacks, he ordered progress be stepped up on the defenses.

As the Germans scrambled to prepare for the massive onslaught ahead, no one knew they were fighting ghosts. General Patton's FUSAG existed only on paper. The tanks the German pilots saw in their passes over England were inflated balloons, the artillery guns made of plywood; the large divisions supposedly attached to the group were really only a handful of units. To support what the German pilots saw, the Allies created huge amounts of information and radio traffic detailing the strength of the phantom armies and the plans for invasion. Captured German spies were turned into double agents and used to send this false information to the Nazi intelligence community.

This greatest of deceptions would succeed beyond the Allies wildest dreams. The Germans not only focused their best divisions in the Pas de Calais, but believed so strongly that the Allies would land there, that even after weeks of fighting in Normandy, those units would still be there, waiting for an attack that never came when they could have driven the landing force in Normandy back to the sea.

Security around Operation Overlord was airtight. Few knew where and when the attack would take place before June 5. Even as the ships loaded with young men sailed for France, many onboard, including most officers, believed they were simply on another training exercise.

As the invasion date drew closer, additional security measures were taken. On May 25, all mail deliveries were frozen. Soon afterward Allied soldiers were confined to their bases. At the beginning of June, the loading of men and equipment began. Practically all of southern England was set in motion, as over 150,000 troops moved from their bases across the island to the vast armada of ships that awaited them along the coast of the English Channel. Seven thousand Allied ships had been gathered for Overlord. A combination of battleships, troop transports, and supply ships crowded the harbors. As these ships were loaded with ammunition, men, and landing craft, they made their way out to the open sea and formed up into their assigned units. By June 3, with everything in place, the invasion seemed ready to go. But a new problem had already arisen, in the form of an enemy that Eisenhower, commander of the greatest invasion fleet in history, could not hope to combat.

The peaceful May weather had disappeared with the month as a massive storm front moved in. The bad weather came gradually at first, but by June 4, the entire English Channel was engulfed with high winds, dark clouds, and pounding rain. Many Allied ships had to retreat back to their harbors and bays for shelter. Any attempted landing in these conditions was guaranteed to be a disaster. Though the situation seemed bleak, Eisenhower decided to wait for updated weather predictions in hope that he wouldn't have to call off the invasion altogether. That evening Captain James Stagg, the Allied meteorologist, gave his final analysis. He predicted that there would be a short break in the weather on June 6. On that day the wind and seas would be calmer, making the invasion possible. But this window, Stagg said, would not last longer than 24 hours; then the terrible conditions would return, and it was unclear when they would again subside. When Stagg finished, it became clear that Eisenhower had only two options: launch the invasion on June 6 and hope the weather would hold long enough for his troops to secure the beaches, or postpone the invasion altogether. Both choices carried enormous risk. If the invasion went forward as planned, the weather might not remain calm enough for sufficient men and equipment to get ashore. That meant the troops that landed could be cut off from resupply and reinforcements, dooming operation Overlord, costing the Allies the element of surprise, and setting back invasion plans for months. If the landing were to be postponed, it would be two weeks before the tide conditions were again suitable for the invasion. Two weeks, during which the Germans might uncover the Allied plan and Overlord would be over before it had the chance to begin. It was these terrible possibilities that swarmed in Eisenhower's head as he considered his choices. Hoping the thoughts of his commanders might help him decide, he asked each one in the room for their opinion. After he had asked every commander, the room was quiet, with the exception of the howling wind and pounding rain, that had become the cause of the tense atmosphere inside. All eyes were on the Allied Supreme Commander, American General Dwight Eisenhower, whose tired face expressed the heavy burden of the decision he now confronted. Every man had been given the chance to voice his opinion, half saying "Yes," the rest saying "No." But ultimately the final decision lay with Eisenhower alone. After a few moments of anxious silence, he spoke. "All right," he said "let's go."

Operation Overlord was a go. On the night of June 5, thousands of troop transports, battleships, and naval craft of every shape and size imaginable departed from England and sailed for the Continent. Overhead, thousands of Allied aircraft took to the skies, carrying the paratroopers that would be the first wave of the attack. Three airborne divisions, the American 101st and 82nd along with the British 6th, were to land south of the targeted beaches and block German reinforcements moving toward the landing point. The paratroopers began landing shortly after midnight and were almost immediately confronted by disaster. Cloud cover hampered the pilots' vision as thick antiaircraft fire, known as flack, illuminated the sky, coming in barrages so thick many of the paratroopers would later say "you could get out and walk on it." In the chaos and confusion, many pilots got lost, dropping paratroopers far from their objectives. For many paratroopers, the problems began when they landed on the ground, because some didn't land on it. The Germans had flooded many of the open fields throughout Normandy, so what looked like solid ground to reconnaissance pilots was actually several feet of water. The paratroopers who landed in these flooded fields were underwater before they knew what was happening. Weighed down by over 100 pounds of equipment and entangled in their parachutes, many drowned. The survivors of the German traps were scattered around the countryside. Slowly working their way through unfamiliar territory, and surrounded by enemy forces, the individual paratroopers began to work their way toward their objectives, organizing themselves into small groups as they came in contact with each other. Men from different platoons, regiments, even different divisions, banded together to seize the closest bridge or city they had been assigned to take.

Firefights erupted across the Normandy peninsula as the disorganized paratroopers engaged individual German units. At around five in the morning, the Americans liberated Sainte-Mère-Eglise, a key town just south of the landing beaches, the first French city to be liberated by the Allies. As the paratroopers were beginning to seize their objectives, the vast armada of battleships and destroyers began to pound the coastline, striking German defenses on the beaches. Then, as dawn broke, American, British, and Canadian soldiers strapped on their gear, swung over the railings of the transport ships, and began to climb down the massive rope ladders to tiny landing craft below. Called Higgins boats, these tiny seacraft had a large ramp at the front that would fall down when the boat hit shore and allow the soldiers onboard to rush onto the beach. The men climbed into these tiny boats as they bobbed in the rolling seas and sprays of salt water splashed on their occupants. Though nervous and seasick, as dawn broke, the young soldiers began to sail toward the beaches. The Normandy coast was divided into five landing areas that would be seized by different Allied divisions.

The British would land on two beaches code named Gold and Sword, while the Canadians landed at Juno in between them. These forces would then combine and seize the city of Caen, a major rail junction, whose capture would open the door to an advance toward Paris. Meanwhile the Americans would land farther to the west at Utah and Omaha beaches and begin to work their way to the port of Cherbourg, which the Allies needed to be able to properly supply the landing force. At around 6:30 AM, the first wave hit the beaches. One of most thoroughly planned and detailed invasions in history now met the ultimate test.

On Sword beach, the farthest east landing site, British troops encountered only light resistance, but it was enough to slow them down and prevent them from reaching Caen, which the Germans scrambled to reinforce.

On Juno and Gold beaches, the British and Canadians faced heavy opposition by well-dug-in German positions. The first wave of Canadians at Juno suffered 50% casualties. It was only through sheer determination and the support of Sherman tanks arriving on shore that the divisions were able to overcome the Germans and advance inland.

Though the fighting at Gold and Juno proved fierce, Omaha beach, the eastern of the two American landing sites, would become infamous for the brutality and chaos of the combat. With large, steep bluffs overlooking the beach, the Germans, in their concrete bunkers equipped with heavy machine guns and large artillery guns, turned the landing site into a kill zone. Some transports were sunk by German artillery on the way to shore. Though some men managed to swim to shore, others were weighed down by their equipment in deep water and drowned. Those that made it to shore were caught in heavy enemy fire, which killed many as they rushed down the ramp of their landing craft. Disorganized, pinned down, and taking heavy losses, the assault fell apart almost immediately. By midday, the American commanders were considering abandoning the landing.

But gradually, the tenacity of the American determination turned the tide, and slowly, and at great cost, they managed to establish a fragile toehold as the sun set.

On a large cliff just west of Omaha beach, another vicious battle raged to protect the American landing. Called Pointe du Hoc, this rocky sea cliff was the location of many German coastal guns overlooking Omaha beach. To neutralize the threats these weapons posed, the American 2nd Ranger Regiment deployed from their ships an hour before the main landings to capture the Pointe. Exiting their landing craft, the Rangers began to scale the 100 -foot cliff while naval artillery soared over their heads forcing the Germans at the top of the cliff, who otherwise would have been firing down at the Rangers, to seek cover. As the first Americans finished the seemingly impossible climb, the real fight began.

Working their way through heavy enemy fire the Rangers gradually pushed forward. But when they approached the location where the coastal artillery was supposed to be, they couldn't find them. Unknown to the Rangers, the Germans had moved the guns less than 48 hours before the attack. Undaunted, they began to push inland in search of their objective. Later in the day, the Rangers found the coastal guns, nearly a mile away from where they were supposed to be, and destroyed them.

At Utah beach, the westernmost landing site of the invasion, the Americans had much better luck than at Omaha. Even the fact that the tides caused the invasion force to land at the wrong location proved to be a good thing. The area where they landed had fewer defenses than the intended landing site. Encountering few enemy troops and quickly pushing inland, they took almost all their D-Day objectives and began linking up with the paratroopers scattered throughout the area.

As the sun set on June the 6th, known as the longest day, four of the five beachheads were secure, only Omaha and the Rangers at Pointe du Hoc were in danger of being pushed back into the sea. Fresh troops and supplies were landing at all the beaches at an astonishing rate. But the Allies had failed to capture all their objectives for D-Day, many of which had proved to be too ambitious, and German reinforcements were pouring into Normandy. D-Day had been a fight. But the real Battle of France had hardly begun.

The Allies still faced a formable task. The Germans were well entrenched across the entire line, and the terrain of Normandy proved to greatly favor the defender. Large trees, narrow dirt roads, and worst of all the hedgerows made Normandy a nightmare for the Allies attempting to break out from their beachhead. To the pre-invasion reconnaissance pilots, the hedgerows looked like small bushes, harmless vegetation. In reality, the hedgerows were centuries-old massive plants, with branches so thickly clustered and roots so strong they could stop a tank in its tracks. It was impossible to remove or pass through these walls of vegetation, confining the Allies' advance to the narrow roads and open fields, perfect kill zones for the German defenders. The Allies suffered heavy casualties as they struggled to advance inland. The British and Canadians were in a deadlocked stalemate with the Germans around Caen, and the Americans were moving at a crawling pace toward Cherbourg. Finally, on June 18, the Americans reached the southern side of the peninsula, cutting off the Germans at Cherbourg. As the enemies' supplies dwindled, the advance picked up, and after a brief siege, Cherbourg capitulated on June 30. But before the Germans surrendered, they had destroyed the port's facilities, and it would not be until August that it would be operational again. This dealt a serious blow to the already damaged Allied supply lines, as the Mulberry ports, which had been towed across the Channel and assembled, had been destroyed in a terrible storm on June 19. Amazingly June 19 was the day Operation Overlord would have been rescheduled if the invasion on the 6th been called off, leaving people to wonder to this day how drastically the invasion of France, and indeed the outcome of the war, might have changed had Eisenhower decided to postpone the attack.

While the Americans were taking Cherbourg in the west, the British were locked in a bitter struggle for Caen in the east. Located where the Normandy peninsula connected with mainland France, the town's capture would give the Allies a launching point for a breakout into western Europe. this is why the Germans fought so bitterly to hold it. Field Marshal Montgomery had made Caen the key objective for D-Day., but after a month of fighting, and several major offensives, it still remained in

German hands. With the British efforts frustrated, the Allies drew up a new plan. Montgomery's forces would continue their bloody fight for Caen while the Americans, having taken Cherbourg, would strike south and try to break through the German flank. Leading this new offensive was General George Patton, who had secretly arrived in France at the end of July. (The Germans still thought he was leading the invasion of Calais that would never come.) Taking command of the newly formed Third Army, Patton's attack began on August 1. Capitalizing on the American victory at St. Lo, his forces broke through the weakened German lines. With the bulk of the German focres pinned down near Caen, there was nothing stopping the Americans from escaping the confining roads of Normandy and moving into the open fields of France. The Allied Blitzkrieg had begun.

While some units fanned out to the south and east to seize Brittany, the bulk of the Third Army cut deep into France before turning North and moving back towards Caen. The Germans now realized the trap the Allies had laid. All their forces in the Normandy area, some 100,000 men, now threatened to be encircled between Patton's army in the west and Montgomery's troops in the east. With it now obvious that the Allies never intended to launch an invasion at the Pas de Calais, the reserves that had been sitting there for months were finally released to Normandy. Though it was too late for them to reverse the German defeats, the commanders hoped to use the reinforcements as a shield for the troops in danger of being surrounded to withdraw to the River Seine, a much better defensive position. But there was one problem with the German strategy, a flaw that appeared it almost all their plans, Hitler.

The Fuhrer refused to even think of withdrawing the troops from Normandy; they were to fight for every square inch of ground. Though his commanders protested, they could not change his mind, and Hitler sealed his army's fate.

With battles wreaking havoc behind their lines, the Germans around Caen began to crack under the intense British pressure. On August 6th, two months later than originally planned, Caen finally fell. This opened the door for a British breakout, and soon they pushed through the crumbling German resistance to link up with Patton's Army. The Germans now found themselves backed into a corner, with the Allies in Normandy to the west and Patton's Army to the south and east. If Montgomery and Patton were able to join forces north of their position, they would be completely surrounded. Despite his commander's pleading for a withdrawal, Hitler ordered the exact opposite, a counterattack. The Allied code breakers quickly discovered the German plans listening to German radio traffic, giving the troops in the targeted area plenty of time to prepare.

With yet another disastrous attack and the Allies swiftly tightening the noose around the Germans, Hitler finally caved to the pressure and for one of the only times in the entire war, ordered his encircled men to retreat. But it appeared too late, with the Allies on the verge of linking up around the town of Falaise. However, the Allies' advance would halt as Patton and Montgomery's armies drew closer, not because of intensified resistance, but due to orders from Montgomery, who was commander of all Allied ground forces. Afraid of his own success, Montgomery feared the British and American troops, advancing rapidly toward each other, might mistake one another for the enemy. The nightmare scenario was a massive firefight between the two armies, with Allied soldiers killing each other.

To prevent this, the Americans were ordered to halt at Argetan, and were to wait for the British, still slogging through tough resistance, to reach them. This left an opening in the encirclement that desperate German troops surged through, while others were able to push through weak points in the Allied lines and escape. Finally, on the evening of August 21st, the pocket was finally sealed as a mixed force of British, Canadian, and Free Polish forces linked up with the American troops. Between 80,000 and 100,000 German troops, over half the entire army in Normandy, was trapped, and those escaping had been forced to abandon most of their equipment.

As the Allies closed the pocket at Falaise, Operation Dragoon, the amphibious invasion of southern France, began on August 15, with troops launched from Italy. Dragoon and Falaise combined were a death knell for the Germans in France. On August 19, the French resistance rose up in Paris. Fearing the Germans would use the rebellion as a reason to burn Paris to the ground, Eisenhower rushed troops toward the capital. Knowing there was nothing to stop the Allies; Hitler ordered his General in Paris to destroy the city before it could be liberated. But it would not be so. Not wanting to be remembered as the man who destroyed one of the world's most beautiful cities, the general refused the Fuhrer's orders. But the battle for Paris lasted in the form of off-and-on skirmishes until the evening of August 24, when a combined Free French and American force joined the Rebels. By the next morning, they had liberated the City of Light.

By early September, the Allies were storming into Belgium, seizing the port of Antwerp, the only one besides Cherbourg that the Germans had not destroyed. But the Germans still occupied the small islands surrounding the port, and their artillery made the area dangerous for ships. They would have to be cleared before the port could be used.

With Antwerp unusable, the Allied armies began to run out of supplies as they entered southern Holland and approached the German border. It wasn't because the supplies weren't available; they just couldn't get it to the frontline units. All supplies had to be shipped from England to Cherbourg, all the way back in Normandy, and then driven hundreds of miles to the frontlines in eastern France and Belgium. It was impossible for the advance to continue until a stockpile could be built up in France and Antwerp made safe to operate in. The Allies ran into additional problems as they reached the recently reinforced German West Wall, better known as the Siegfried line. With the massive defensive network on the prewar German border, the Germans were able to reorganize a strong defense in the fortifications, further slowing the Allied advance. With the lack of supplies and stiffening German resistance, the Allies were running out of options. It seemed their only viable choice would be to halt and dig in for the winter, using the time to reorganize and resupply. The offensive could not be renewed until spring, meaning the war would drag on into 1945.

But Montgomery was not ready to accept that just yet, and he proposed an ambitious, high-risk plan that had extreme odds against success. But if it did succeed, it might just end the war by Christmas.

The plan Montgomery put forward, code-named operation Market Garden, was to concentrate the Allied offensive in a single thrust into the Netherlands. The 2nd Army, under Montgomery's command would push into northern Holland and then turn east, outflanking the Siegfried line (which reached only to the northern border of Belgium) and striking into the heart of Germany. Market Garden faced two key problems. One, the supplies needed to pull it off were much more than Montgomery's troops had available. Second, the British would have to cross several rivers to be in a position to outflank the Siegfried line, and the Germans were guaranteed to blow up these bridges if the Allies tried to cross. Montgomery argued that both challenges could be overcome. The supplies needed to carry out the operation were available, just not in his army. Therefore, he asked Eisenhower to increase his troops' stockpile at the expense of the others, and the Allies could prevent the Germans from destroying the bridges they needed to cross by dropping paratroopers behind enemy lines to seize the bridges ahead of time.

Some commanders argued Montgomery's plan wouldn't work because it was too ambitious or just too ridiculous to work. But Eisenhower wanted to keep the Germans under as much pressure as possible to prevent them from reorganizing, and, he thought, if the operation were a success, the war might really be over.

On September 17, 1944, Operation Market Garden began with the largest airborne drop the world had seen up to that point. From the south, Montgomery's forces began to advance toward the bridges. The American 101st airborne division landed near the town of Eindhoven, the southernmost landing location. Meeting little resistance, they quickly secured four of the five bridges, but were unable to stop the Germans from destroying the fifth. Farther north and deeper into German territory, the 82nd airborne landed at Nijmegen. Miscommunication between the divisions delayed their attack on the targeted bridge, giving the Germans vital time to organize a defense. It took three days of bloody fighting before the 82nd finally took the bridge on September 20. The landing farthest from Allied lines was made by the British 1st airborne division at the city of Arnhem, though Allied intelligence had reported shortly before the landings began that two German Panzer divisions were stationed near Arnhem. The Allied commanders decided to go ahead as planned, believing the Germans were too weak in the Netherlands to prevent them from reaching their objectives. It would prove to be a terrible underestimation. The British paratroopers were scattered into disorganized groups by heavy enemy fire. Only a small, isolated force reached the bridge, managing to secure half of it, while the Germans prevented them from seizing the rest. Though reinforcements and supplies were dropped to all three divisions, the paratroopers couldn't hold out by themselves forever, and it was the job of the British XXX corps spearheading the army's advance to link up with them.

Though the XXX corps attack north was suppose to be swift and relatively easy, this soon proved not to be the case. All the divisions had to advance down a down highway 69, a two-lane road that became known as Hell's Highway. This confined and predictable path made it easy for the Germans to concentrate their forces along the highway, and almost immediately the dash toward the airborne troops became a crawl. It was predicted that the British would reach the 101st at Eindhoven on the first day. Instead it took four, a severe blow to the timetable of Market Garden, as the British were supposed to have reached Arnhem by now. Every hour that XXX corps was held up, the danger that the paratroopers at Nijmegen and Arnhem would be overrun increased. Though the British reached Nijmegen in relatively short order, German counterattacks and supply problems continued to hamper the British advancement toward their ultimate objective; the bridge over the Rhine at Arnhem. By the time they approached the south side of the river on September 25, it was too late. The British 1st airborne division had been all but annihilated and had lost control of the bridge. Surrounded, beaten, and running low on everything, the exhausted paratroopers, under the cover of darkness, were ferried across to the Allied bank. Of the nearly 11,000 men dropped on September 17, barely 2,300 managed to escape. The rest were either killed or taken prisoner. The 1st airborne division would never recover. Operation Market Garden had failed. With no chance of ending the war in 1944, Allied armies everywhere began to halt and dig in as the temperature dropped. But as a lull in the fighting began, along the Belgian-German border, in the Ardennes forest nearly 250,000 German troops and 1,000 tanks were assembling in absolute secrecy. Though winter might be closing in, the war in Europe was about to heat up.

Don Dill
May 22, 1924 – February 17, 2010

Don Dill was born on May 22, 1924, in south Delaware County, Ohio. Like every childhood, there were both good and bad events for him and his family. Don found school easy and made many friends, because he was not hard to get along with. Don spent his early years in a farmhouse overlooking his father's farm. But life in that house ended when his father heard the dogs while milking cows one night. When he went to investigate, he discovered the house had caught on fire with the rest of his family inside. Although everyone made it out, the house burned down and the Dills lost all their possessions with it. Don's father and grandfather went to a local lumber company and bought a kit house that had to be put together. They hired local carpenters to help put the house together, but it took time, and while the house was under construction the family had to live in their garage. Sleeping on the dirty, hard floor every night and having little space or privacy, Don and his family did their best to make it home until they could move into the new house. It was a relief when they moved into the new house with more space and new furniture and something not even their old house had electricity.

When the United States entered WWII, all men between ages 18 and 45 were drafted unless they were excused for some other purpose. Don was one of the three men in Franklin County who received a farm deferment, allowing him to stay and work on his family farm due to a shortage of farm labor. Don worked on his family's farm until late 1944, when the government decided to take away his deferment and draft him. He was forced to say good-bye to his family and farm and head for Camp Little Rock, Arkansas. He didn't care what branch of the military they sent him to, and ended up as an infantryman.

When the Battle of the Bulge began, the need for replacements became urgent. Although his training had not been completed, Don and his comrades were surprised when they were ordered to pack quickly and were rushed out of camp to the shore. From there they were shipped across the Atlantic to France. Once in Europe the green Americans found themselves on their way to the Bulge area. Don found the terrain and weather in the Ardennes to be harsh. The weather often dipped well below zero, and the snow was deep and crusty. Although many soldiers could just walk on top of the snow, Don, carrying his heavy BAR (Browning automatic rifle), sunk and found it hard to keep up with the others. Despite the constant movement and activity while in Europe, Don still had time to make friends. One fellow soldier he quickly became close to was a man named David Jones. Becoming fast friends, they took turns watching all their gear while the other slept. But when David was assigned to another unit heading for a different area of the front, the two men were forced to split up. Don did not hear from David for the rest of the war. Not until he returned did Don find David's name and address in his address book. Eager to reconnect with his friend, Don sent him a letter asking how he was doing. it did not take long for a return letter to come. It revealed a mind-blowing shock for Don. David Jones had been killed in Europe shortly after reaching his new assignment. Don sent a letter to and later met David's parents and they shared stories of the man they greatly missed.

Don found the intensity and fear combat could bring when the sergeant ordered his squad to spread out and advance into the woods. As they moved out, bullets started flying, and machine gun fire broke out on their flank. The Americans took cover and fired back. Although they managed to fend off their attackers, Don thought it had been stupid of the sergeant not to tell them that he was sending them out to combat. Don didn't remain on the frontline for long after that. In February 1945 he joined four other men on a daylight patrol during a heavy snowstorm. When they set up a position later that day by digging several foxholes, they assigned one man the first watch. He was the nervous one of the group, always worried about combat. Don himself rarely got worried and commented later, "Maybe I was too dumb to be scared." The man assigned lookout, however, didn't take his watch, and stayed in a fox hole with Don complaining about the cold. Not wanting to argue or give any nearby Germans any chance of a surprise attack, Don decided to be the lookout himself. And good thing he did! No sooner had he exited the hole than he heard talking and saw figures nearby. Knowing they were Germans, he raised his BAR and began firing, He doesn't know how many he took down, but he took several. The Germans fired back and soon a firefight broke out. One single German bullet flew down the barrel of Don's gun, and the blast knocked him back and took off part of his trigger finger. That firefight was Don's last. When the men reported back to base, the sergeant decided he had been too injured to stay, and Don took an ambulance to Paris and then a C-47 plane to England. Despite his injuries, Don had no desire to leave. As he said himself, "I would have liked to stay. I wasn't a hero, but I wasn't ready to quit the war."

Don returned to America later in 1945. When he returned home, he tried going to college and learn accounting, but decided to return to farming. He married, and, with help from his father built a second house for him and his new wife on the farm. Don worked on his family's farm until 1960, when he started his own construction company, working with 3 other men. They worked together for many years building and remodeling houses. They avoided injury and even constructed a 1.7 million dollar house. Don retired in 1986 after running the company for 26 years.

Looking back on his service Don is proud to have served in the U.S. military.

Wendell Ellenwood
January 14, 1922 -

Born in Jackson County, Ohio, on January 14, 1922, Wendell Ellenwood grew up with a love of horseback riding, which he became very good at while growing up on his family's farm.

After starting college at Ohio State University in 1940, Wendell joined ROTC (Reserve Officer Training Corps) program and became part of the Army's reserve force. After the Japanese attacked Pearl Harbor and the United States entered World War II, ROTC sent Wendell to be trained for active duty at Fort Sill, Oklahoma. After receiving a commission as a corporal and assigned to the 752nd Field Artillery Battalion, Wendell took the dangerous job of a forward observer. After completing training with the 752nd, he prepared to deploy to Europe. Before leaving, Wendell married his girlfriend, Mary Janet, and then bid good-bye to his loved ones as he headed out to the uncertainty of war.

Deployed to Europe in 1944, Wendell landed at Utah Beach along the Normandy coast and joined the Allies in the fight to liberate France from German control. As a forward observer, Wendell spent most of his time on the frontlines with the infantry units, using his radio to direct artillery fire on the enemy. With the constant motion of battle, he never spent much time in one place, going wherever the artillery went. During the long months on the front lines, Wendell had many close encounters with the enemy. The most memorable for him was during an engagement in a small woods in Western Europe. The Americans were struggling, held up at the edge of an open field because the Germans were firing at them from the other side. While taking fire, Wendell directed his unit's artillery guns from the limited protection of his foxhole. The American guns gave the Germans such a pounding that they soon were signaling their surrender. Wendell crossed the field with the infantry. After securing the prisoners, he took them back to an American post and turned them over to Army interrogators. But Wendell received a reminder that the victory was only a small one. Just as he left the American dug-out to return to the front, they were suddenly shelled by German artillery, forcing Wendell and the others to take cover as shrapnel rained around them.

On December 16, 1944, the Germans launched a final, desperate offensive in the Ardennes forest to try to reverse the course of the war. The Battle of the Bulge, the largest land battle the Allies would ever fight, had begun. Fought during the coldest winter Europe had experienced in nearly 100 years, frostbite and hypothermia cost the Allies nearly as many casualties as enemy action. With his unit among those organized to halt the attack, Wendell spent over a month in these horrible conditions, calling in artillery on any German units he spotted, which were in abundance. Years later, when reflecting on his experiences in the Bulge, Wendell still can't help feeling surprised he survived.

Following the German surrender and the end of World War II, 1st Lieutenant Wendell Ellenwood returned to the United States in December 1945. Immediately after disembarking the ship, he found a phone and called his family, who were overjoyed to hear he was coming home. The family reunion was a happy one, especially for Wendell and Mary, who had been apart for most of their nearly two years of marriage.

Following his discharge from the military Wendell became the Director of the Ohio Union at Ohio State University. He and Mary Janet started a family, raising four kids; Sandy, Dean, Kay, and Gary. The family has now grown to include 7 grandchildren and 1 great-grandchild.

For his service, Lieutenant Wendell Ellenwood received the Purple Heart, The Bronze Star with a V (the V stands for Valor), the Air Medal, the French Croix De Guerre, and the French Liberation Medal. Wendell is proud to have fought and survived the Battle of the Bulge. But with the pride is also the sadness of having been away from his family for over two years and the knowledge that he had to kill people during the war. Despite this, Wendell is still proud to have been part of the Allied cause, and wants everyone to remember that World War II was a war to free the people of Europe.

In the Heat of Winter

O N THE COLD, FOGGY, MORNING of December 16, 1944, in the thick woods of the Ardennes forest, the starting point for the German Blitzkrieg into France four years earlier, the final, decisive battle of World War II began. As German tanks rolled down the narrow dirt roads and German infantry marched through the snow, what was supposedly a "quiet area" of the frontline became the site of the largest battle the U.S. Army ever fought. Two hundred and fifty thousand of Hitler's crack troops, and 1,000 of the Nazis' best tanks, faced only 80,000 American soldiers, many fresh from training, and the rest weary from months or years of fighting, with only a handful of armored units available. At stake was nothing less than the outcome of the Second World War and the fate of humanity.

Three months before the beginning of this climactic battle, in spite of strained supply lines and the failure of Operation Market Garden, the Allied armies continued to advance toward the German Fatherland. On October 21, after 19 days of heavy fighting, Aachen became the first major German city to fall into Allied hands. Parts of the German Siegfried line were in danger of being overrun, and with the ongoing war against the Soviet Union, there weren't enough replacements for the massive casualties the Germans had suffered in France.

With such a dire position, the German commanders were preparing for a last-ditch defense along the Siegfried line, using every available weapon and man to hold off the Allies. Unlike the previous German strategies, this one had no end game. The plan was simply to delay the inevitable Allied victory for as long as possible, for everyone except Hitler and his most fanatical followers knew the war was lost. But because he didn't see it that way, the Fuhrer wasn't satisfied with a solely defensive strategy. He wanted an offensive, one that, in his mind, would give the Third Reich a chance to reverse the course of events. The plan Hitler presented to his generals was more daring and wildly ambitious than anything the Germans had attempted since the initial invasion of the Soviet Union. The plan called for a massive Blitzkrieg through the Ardennes Forest, and across Belgium to the newly opened port of Antwerp along the English Channel. The Germans would destroy the port, dealing a death blow to Allied supply lines and cutting off Montgomery's forces in Holland from the Americans in France. The physical division of the Allied armies would divide the already shaky Anglo-American alliance. Unable to get along politically, Britain and America would be unable to continue the war and be forced to sue for peace. With the war in the west over, the Germans could turn their full energies to the Soviet Union and halt if not reverse their advance toward Berlin.

This was the offensive and outcome Hitler envisioned. His generals were mortified. They argued that they didn't have the manpower and resources to launch the attack and that the risk was too great. Everything would have to break their way for the Germans to reach Antwerp, not to mention surviving the Allied counterattacks. They also knew that believing the offensive would break up the British-American Alliance was wishful dreaming at best. They begged Hitler to abandon the plan, but as always, he ignored them.

Code-named Operation Watch on the Rhine, a deceptive name used to make the Allies believe the Germans were organizing a new defensive plan;

preparation for the attack was under a cloak of secrecy. The German plan benefited from the cloudy winter weather, which blinded Allied pilots to their activity, and from the fact that, unlike in France and other German-occupied territories, there were no resistance organizations inside the Fatherland to spy on and report troop movements. Several army intelligence officers warned that the Germans were capable of launching a major offensive, and even predicted the Ardennes as the target area. But with such limited information, many Allied leaders dismissed their warnings. One general did not ignore the intelligence reports, and this would prove decisive in the approaching battle.

At 0530 hours on the morning of December 16, 1944, operation Watch on the Rhine was put into action, and the Battle of the Bulge began. One Thousand and six hundred German artillery guns opened fire on Allied positions in the Ardennes. Overhead, Germany's few remaining airborne units parachuted behind Allied lines to seize the Baraque Michael crossroads for the advancing assault. Meanwhile, a small group of German soldiers, dressed in the uniforms of captured Americans, walked casually through Allied checkpoints. Once behind American lines, they began spreading disinformation, switching street signs, and wreaking all kinds of havoc. Along the frontline, German troops marched down the same paths they had four years earlier in the invasion of France. Caught completely by surprise, the American positions collapsed, and the Germans advanced rapidly. Thick clouds prevented the dominant Allied air force from supporting the desperate troops on the ground, and within 48 hours, two of three American divisions stationed in the Ardennes had been virtually destroyed, and the survivors were being routed. With the Germans once again advancing into Belgium, they created a bulge in the Allied line, giving the battle its name. With his forces reeling in shock at the unfolding catastrophe, Eisenhower immediately assembled his generals. Though the situation was dire, Eisenhower saw the German attack as an opportunity to destroy Hitler's best divisions. Turning to Patton, the Supreme Commander asked how long it would take him to organize his army, located south of the German offensive, for a counterattack. Patton, to the disbelief of everyone, said his troops could launch the attack in a mere 48 hours. Nobody believed him, but they didn't know Patton's secret. His chief intelligence officer was among those who had predicted the German attack in advance. Patton, heeding his warning, already had plans for a counterattack in place. He was simply waiting for the order, which he now had. In addition to Patton's army, Eisenhower ordered additional reinforcements to block the German advance from the front, and Montgomery's troops in Holland to attack from the North. But these plans would take time to execute, and the Germans needed to be stopped now. To buy the counterattacking forces time to prepare, Eisenhower did the one thing he knew had a chance of slowing the German advance. He ordered the 101st airborne division to deploy to Bastogne.

A small town situated on a ridge in the Ardennes forest, Bastogne seemed like just another ordinary town, but its strategic value was immeasurable. The reason was that all seven of the major roads in the Ardennes area ran through this small town. In such a rural region, this made the control of the town a must. Whoever controlled Bastogne controlled the roads. The Germans were fast approaching Bastogne, their advance delayed only by bitter resistance from isolated American units. But this bought the paratroopers enough time to establish defensive positions inside the town, and they fended off the initial German attack. Though the capture of Bastogne was critical to the success of the German attack, so was speed. Trying to achieve both, the German commander had his forces surround Bastogne, then continue the advance, leaving one Panzer regiment and a Grenadier division to seize the vital crossroads. On December 20, the last road leading out of Bastogne was seized by the Germans, and the Siege of Bastogne began. Although outnumbered, outgunned, and severely limited on supplies, the Americans in Bastogne proved extremely stubborn in their resistance beating back all German probes and assaults.

Bastogne was not the only place the Germans were encountering stiffening resistance. Almost everywhere, individual American units were fighting with incredible tenacity. Individual units would hold up an entire division for hours, and engineers blew up bridges as the Germans approached, the capture of every village. Every Allied position, was taking too long. The massacres of American prisoners, most infamously at Malmedy, deepened the determination of every American soldier to fight. The German spearhead units were also starting to encounter supply problems. With the Americans still holding out in Bastogne, it was becoming impossible for the Germans to resupply the troops leading the advance. To top off the German problems, Patton, true to his word, had already begun his counterattack at the southern edge of the bulge, threatening to break through to the encircled Americans at Bastogne. If he succeeded, the Germans would be unable to supply and reinforce the troops west of the town, and any chance of success would be lost. With this in mind, the Germans prepared to launch the largest attack on Bastogne yet, with the goal of crushing the

Americans who remained. But still hoping for a faster, less costly solution, the German commander sent General Anthony McAulliffe, commander of the Americans in the besieged town, a formal demand of surrender. It is hard to say what the German commander expected the American reply to be, but he probably never imagined it to be anything like what he received. The American messenger delivered the formal reply; the letter had just one word: "NUTS!" Confused and enraged, the commander asked the American messenger what it meant. "It means go to hell!" the messenger said. Not amused by the American response, on Christmas Eve the Germans launched their assault.

At first, the attack seemed to be successful when the Germans penetrated the American perimeter. But the initial victory turned into a stalemate as the Americans fought back with everything they had. Both Panzer columns were destroyed and the advance ground to a halt. Reeling from their losses, the Germans were thrown back to their starting position. The Americans in Bastogne had survived.

With Christmas day came a new spirit throughout the Allied ranks. The tide of the Battle of the Bulge was changing, the fight shifting from one of survival to offensive. The skies were beginning to clear, and as they did, were filled with Allied fighters and bombers. The Allied aircraft targeted German supply vehicles, easy targets in the confined, narrow roads of the Ardennes. Soon the German advance, quite literally, ran out of fuel. Fresh supplies could be dropped into Bastogne, and Allied troops everywhere again had their dominant air support. The German advance toward Antwerp stalled before reaching as far as the Meuse River. Many units literally ran out of fuel, and the rest were halted by the

British and American troops arriving from all over Europe. In the south, Patton's Third Army finally broke through the German flank, and on December 26, lifted the siege of Bastogne.

With the liberation of Bastogne went any hope of a German victory. Back on the offensive, the Allies began to take back the German gains. In some places, the retreating enemy put in bitter resistance to the end, while other units surrendered or routed in droves. The Germans who managed to escape the Allied grasp were forced to leave behind much of their heavy equipment, leaving tanks abandoned on the roadsides and big guns in their positions. By January 25, 1945, all German troops were back where they had started almost six weeks earlier and in far worse shape than before. The Battle of the Bulge was over.

The casualties were terrible on both sides. Over 80,000 American troops were casualties, 19,000 of whom had been killed and over 20,000 others now faced the horrors of German prison camps. One Thousand four hundred British troops were killed, wounded, or captured. Many men lay in hospitals not because of enemy action, but due to the severe Ardennes winter. It would take many a long time to recover; some never would. But if the Allied losses were tragic, German losses were catastrophic. Though nobody has ever come up with an accurate number, estimates range from 70,000 to 100,000 German casualties, many of them old men and teenage boys, other were the Reich's most experienced troops. The losses of men and equipment were of a magnitude Germany could never hope to replace. Not only was Soviet pressure in the east mounting, but now, the defenses facing the western Allies were stretched to the limit. The Germans found it impossible to fill the gaps left in their ranks by such crushing losses. Hitler's gamble not only failed to bring Germany a victory, but sealed the fate for its inevitable defeat.

Eddie Leibbrand
January 27, 1924

Edwin "Eddie" Thomas Leibbrand was born on January 27, 1924 in Columbus, Ohio. His father worked hard during the depression to support Eddie, his mother, and three sisters. During his high school years Eddie developed mastoiditus, which forced him to miss a year of school. On January 30, 1943, Eddie was drafted out of high school, and after passing his physical exam on the second try he was sent to Camp Atterbury, Indiana, on March 1 for indoctrination. A week later he headed for Camp Walters, Texas for basic training. After training, Eddie's unit deployed to Alaska, but because of a problem with his eye glasses, Eddie could not go and instead joined the 110th Regiment of the 28th division.

On August 17, 1944 Eddie's unit departed on the Queen Elizabeth for an 8 day voyage to England. Despite the fact that 10,000 soldiers were crammed on the ship, the men may have had been a little spoiled due to entertainment they had from one of Americans most popular singers of the time, Bing Crosby, who was crossing the Atlantic on the ship. After arriving in England, Eddie received several more weeks of training before he and his unit were shipped in Higgins boats across the English Channel to Le Havre, France in September. Eddie then participated in the Allied push to force the Germans back to the Fatherland, helping in the liberation of Belgium and Luxembourg. On December 16, 1944, the German offensive in the Ardennes began. The Germans soon reached the town where Eddie was stationed and brutal fighting broke out. In three days, Eddie's regiment suffered 2,700 casualties while the attacking Germans lost a similar number of men. With the Americans units scattered and disorganized, they asked a local German boy where a good place to regroup would be, not knowing he was a Nazi. The place the boy suggested a nearby field where they found a number of American tanks. But when Eddie and the others arrived they discovered the tanks had been disabled and were ambushed by German soldiers. Many of the men were killed and those left standing had no choice but to surrender. Eddie was among the captured men. For days they were forced to march non-stop with nothing to eat or drink. On one day they were forced to walk in a circle through the same village multiple times to enforce the stories of Nazi at propaganda papers that thousands of Americans had been taken prisoner. The prisoners were then loaded into train cars designed to carry no more than 40 people but sometimes almost 100 were forced in one. They traveled at night to avoid Allied planes, the bathroom was a helmet, and they had no fresh air. Once when a man did manage to open a window and poked his head to out to get fresh air a German guard did not hesitate to kill him. Despite all the hardships, Eddie never lost faith in the Lord, or the power of prayer. Just hours after the whole group prayed together for food, the Germans gave them rations to sustain them.

After arriving at Stalag-9B near Bad Orb, Germany, the men were put to work daily, chopping firewood for nearby residences. Eddie once volunteered for a project just to get a break from the daily routine. The task he was assigned however, was a horrible one. The task was burying the bodies of dead Americans. Eddie never volunteered again. Many men died from starvation, disease, or the cold, as they had no warm clothing. When a German guard was found dead, all the prisoners were lined up in knee deep snow during a freezing cold night and told they were going to stay there until the killer was found. The Germans soon found a prisoner with blood on his cloths and the remainder were allowed back inside. Another brief moment of life threatening excitement came a few months later, while standing in the camp yard Eddie saw a P-47 plane streaking right at him from a low level. Eddie could clearly see the pilots face and also look down the barrel of his .30 caliber machine gun, Eddie thought he was dead. Then at the last possible second the plane pulled away. It had turned out that some of the French prisoners had spelled POW on the ground with limestone and the pilot had seen it just before strafing the camp. The day after Easter tanks from Patton's Third army rolled through the barricades and the German guards surrendered without a fight.

Eddie was finally liberated, but in no condition to celebrate. The harsh conditions had taken their toll on the young man. After one of the liberating soldiers gave the starving prisoner a portion of a military ration, Eddie started to walk away, when he suddenly collapsed. It was impossible for him to stomach even the smallest amount of food. He spent three months in a hospital recovering. When he was strong enough Eddie returned home on board a destroyer, he recalls they were followed the whole way to New York by a German submarine that had surrendered. Eddie and his family reunited in early August 1945. For 60 days they had time to catch up, do activates as a family, and simply enjoy each other's company. In October Eddie's leave expired and he was shipped to Miami Beach for two weeks of R&R. He then followed orders to report to Fort Bragg in North Carolina where he began training for operating a 60 mm mortar in preparation for his deployment to the Pacific theater. Of course, Eddie protested on the grounds he had suffered enough as a POW to deserve a discharge. Two weeks later his request was granted based on the point system and Eddie deployed to Camp Atterbury in Indiana for his final processing out of the military. On his way to Indiana the train stopped in Columbus just a few miles from his family's home. Eddie was heartbroken when told he could not get off the train for a brief visit. Private Eddie Leibbrand was officially discharged from the Army on November 28, 1945.

After his discharge Eddie became a machine repairman for C&O railroad. While at a bingo game, he met a young woman named Billie, and they soon fell in love and married in 1946. They had one son. After ten years working at C&O Eddie became a machinist for Columbus Boltworks, a job he held for 28 years.

In August 1981 Billie died and Eddie remarried in 1983 to Jane, a widow with two daughters whom Eddie has always treated as his own.

Rupert "Twink" Starr
July 16, 1922 -

Rupert Dano "Twink" Starr was born in Mount Sterling, Ohio on July 16, 1922. When he was old enough he joined a local Boy Scout troop and through them discovered he loved camping. Twink enjoyed all the other activities he did with his troop as well, especially being crowd ushers for the local OSU football games. He was three merit badges from being an Eagle Scout.

Just a short distance from Twink's colonial designed house, lived the then-Ohio Governor John Bricker. Often the Governor would come home for the weekends and almost every Sunday Twink could walk down to the Governor's house and see him working of relaxing in the yard. Never a shy kind of guy, Twink would always yell over the fence "Hello Governor!" Twink became so familiar that Governor Bricker changed his response from "Hello young man." to "Hello, Rupert." Twink, as a Boy Scout became a fan of Governor Bricker, and helped as a volunteer during his next campaign.

After graduating high school in 1940, Twink enrolled at Ohio University. By now Europe had been engulfed in war against Hitler's armies for nearly a year, and in Twink's opinion, it was only a matter of time before the United States was drug into the fight. With this in mind, Twink decided to be ready when his country entered the war and he joined the Army ROTC (Reserve Officer Training Corps). Twink turned out to be right; the United States entered the war after the Japanese attack on Pearl Harbor on December 7, 1941. After this, the country needed all the able bodied men it could get, and in September of 1943, Twink and his ROTC class were put on active duty.

Basic Training at Fort Benning, Georgia proved not as difficult as Twink anticipated. The extremely rigorous obstacle course the OU wrestling coach made all ROTC students run was actually more physically demanding than anything he had to do at Fort Benning and Twink passed basic training with ease, becoming part of a new glider infantry unit. Shortly after the unit's creation, it suffered its first casualties. Several men were killed or injured, and gliders destroyed beyond repair, and that was a training exercise. After seeing how many problems the gliders had, and not wanting any more training fatalities, the Army disbanded his glider unit before it was activated and Twink was reassigned to the 422nd Regiment of the 106th Infantry Division.

After completing officer's training Twink received a commission as 2nd Lieutenant and went to Camp Atterbury Indiana. While stationed there, Twink's job was to select Sergeants on the base, to send to Europe to fill leadership vacancies in units that had suffered casualties. Deciding who remained in the Safety of Camp Atterbury and who marched off to war and potentially death was a very burdensome task for the young Lieutenant and he hated every minute of it. Eventually, Twink managed to convince another officer to trade jobs with him, and he happily left the terrible job.

In the fall of 1944, Twink moved with the 106th Division to Camp Miles Standish in Massachusetts and there they boarded a transport ship bound for Scotland. After a long voyage across the Atlantic Ocean, and the soldiers climbed onto the ship's deck to watch as the Scottish shoreline came into view. Nearby, Twink spotted a Beautiful Barge in the harbor with the letters HMS printed in gold along the side. As he admired the wonderful looking ship, Twink saw two figures standing on the deck waving to the troops. As his transport craft sailed by, Twink got a closer look at the figures and couldn't believe his eyes "It's the King and Queen!" he yelled, and soon the whole crowd of soldiers was full of excitement and shouts as everyone attempted to catch a glimpse of King George VI and Queen Elizabeth. To this day Twink tells everyone that the King and Queen met him in the harbor on his first trip to Britain.

After the units royal entrance onto the Island, they traveled south to England and boarded another ship that took them across the Channel to Le Havre France, where they landed on October 27, 1944. Next, Twink and the others took a long truck ride from the French coast to the Belgian German border, where the frontline now was. Traveling through Western Europe, they passed through the sites of many historical World War I battles. The old battlefields were still littered with broken and rusting equipment, standing as a silent reminder of the Great War.

On December 11, Twink's unit took up positions on the frontline in the Ardennes forest, relieving another American unit that had been near the action for a long time. For the first few days, there was little to worry about besides the cold, as the violence. Then on December 16, all hell broke loose as the Germans launched their Ardennes Offensive. Twink and his comrades, having virtually no combat experience, found themselves in the heart of the Battle of the Bulge, the largest battle the US Army has ever fought.

Though the German attack caught everyone off guard Twink and the others fought back tenaciously. But they were outnumbered and overstretched (The 106th only had the manpower to hold 3 miles of the frontline, but was given responsibility for 27 miles the line). Within the first 48 hours, Twink's regiment was completely surrounded. The Commanding Officer gathered Twink and a group of officers and told them of the grim situation. With all lines of communication cut, Division Headquarters needed to be told of their situation. The only way to make contact with them would be for a messenger to travel on foot, through German held territory, and reach the new frontline. It was such a dangerous mission the commander decided he couldn't order any man to take the risk, he asked for volunteers. Nobody moved, for a moment it looked like nobody would volunteer... then Twink Starr stepped forward.

Feeling that it was his job as an officer and a soldier to ensure the men beside him returned safely home, gave Twink the courage to take on this impossible challenge. Not wanting him to go alone, one of the Sergeants stepped forward and volunteered to go with Twink. Together, the two men set off into the freezing, German infested forest in search of the American lines whose location they did not know.

For three days Twink and his comrade cautiously made their way through the Ardennes, searching for fellow Americans while dodging German patrols. But after 72 hours of sneaking through the forest, their luck ran out and they were captured by German troops.

Joining a group of prisoners, they were marched east into Germany. The captured Americans quickly learned that their guards were not the only danger as American bombers continued to enemy targets near their position. After being forced to march most of the way, Twink and his fellow prisoners, were placed in a prison camp in eastern Germany. They remained there for several months, suffering under the harsh Nazi treatment having to survive without bare necessities and only enough food to keep them alive.

Finally, in the early spring of 1945, the worst of Twink's ordeal ended with the arrival of Soviet troops. The Americans were moved to another camp in Germany. Though the Soviets were much kinder than the Germans, the supposedly liberated Americans were kept under armed guard and their movement was still restricted to the Soviet facility. Twink quickly started to feel that he was still a prisoner, despite the Soviet alliance with the US. When Nazi Germany surrendered, the American prisoners were ready to return home. An English ship took them to Italy, where they boarded an American transport bound for the United States and home.

Twink arrived home in the winter of 1945, just in time to celebrate Christmas with his family. After a happy family reunion, 1st Lieutenant Rupert Starr was discharged on January 26, 1946. Returning to civilian life, Mr. Starr started working as Sales Manager for John W. Galbreath a prominent local and national real estate broker estate broker. Finding he liked the business, Mr. Starr eventually went out on his own and made a career through buying and selling real estate.

In 1955, Twink not being able to marry his college girlfriend, met a young man, Allan Wingfield. The two took an instant liking for each other, and they lived together for over 53 years.

For his service 1st Lieutenant Starr received the Combat Infantry Badge, the Bronze Star, The European Theater Medal, The WWII Victory Medal, and the Peace Medal, which is given specifically to prisoners of war. Twink is proud of his courage under enemy fire, but ashamed by the fact he was captured. "For the longest time I never told anybody I was a POW. I felt embarrassed by it. Felt that I should have been killed instead." Twink says. But, after half a century of silence, fellow POWs convinced Twink to march with them in a fourth of July parade in 2009. Twink felt amazed and deeply moved by the applause and obvious respect the crowds gave the former prisoners as they marched by, and since then, much of the shame he once felt is gone, its place filled with pride for what he and his countrymen did.

Twink wants everyone to remember that the veterans of World War II fought hard to preserve our democracy. And that in spite of the German advantages, such as the fighter jet and infamous V-2 rocket, our wonderful military, personal resourcefulness, and home front industry enabled us to overcome all the odds.

Victory in Europe

I N EARLY FEBRUARY 1945, THE Allied forces, reorganized
from the Battle of the Bulge and adequately resupplied
through the newly opened port of Antwerp, launched a
new offensive with the objective of ending the most
terrible war in human history. Realizing they were now
too weak to stop the Allies at the border, the German
commanders asked Hitler for permission to withdraw to
the east bank of the Rhine River. One of the largest rivers
in Germany, it provided a natural barrier against the Allied
Armies, which would ease the pressure on the broken
German army. Hitler refused; as always, he demanded not
an inch of ground be yielded without a fight. It would
prove to be a fatal mistake. As the Allies approached the
river, German engineers blew the bridges. Though this
prevented the Allies from crossing, it also trapped the
German troops still fighting on the west bank, costing
them even more unnecessary losses. And the Germans
didn't get to every bridge first. On March 7, the men of
the 9th Armored division were shocked by what they
discovered while capturing the town of Remagen; a usable
bridge over the Rhine river. Seizing the opportunity, a
small squad rushed across the bridge under heavy fire and
seized a small hill on the other side. Germany's last line of
defense had been breached. When Hitler found out, he
went into a rage, demanding the bridge be destroyed
immediately. The Germans used everything from floating
mines to V-2 rockets, but these proved too inaccurate to
work. Meanwhile the American bridgehead on the east
bank continued to grow, until on March 17, the bridge,
already damaged when the Allies had captured it, suddenly
collapsed. But the loss of the bridge had little impact on

the American advance, as engineers had already constructed several pontoon bridges that continued to allow reinforcements and supplies to pour across the river.

To build on the momentum established at Remagen, on March 22, General Patton's Third Army launched its own river crossing at Oppenheim, pushing six miles inland on day one. On March 24, General Montgomery's forces launched a massive river crossing at the towns of Rees and Wesel. Code-named Operation Varsity, it involved nearly 250,000 men. Now over the formidable Rhine barrier, nothing but the collapsing German army stood between the Allies and victory. Targeting the Ruhr, a region that possessed virtually all of Germany's war industry and production factories, Allied forces moved in. Montgomery's 9th Army in the north, and the American first Army at Remagen to the south, formed two pincers around the industrial area and the nearly 430,000 German troops defending it. Then, on April 1, the groups linked up east of the Ruhr, trapping the Germans in one massive encirclement. Facing mostly SS training units, old men, and boys as young as 12, the Americans encountered a variety of resistance as they slowly liberated the Ruhr, one town at a time. Some units surrendered without firing a shot, while others fought with a fanatical ferocity to the bitter end.

Outside the Ruhr was a similar story. Though most Germans could see the war was over, a few of Hitler's most fanatical followers continued to try to stop the Allied war machine, now sweeping across the Fatherland. But even with victory in sight, Eisenhower and his commanders were concerned that their armies were advancing almost too quickly, and eventually they would meet the Soviets advancing from the east. The fear was the same as that of the Falaise pocket, that the two Allied armies would mistake each other for the enemy, resulting in a tragic bloodbath. To prevent this, Eisenhower declared the Elbe River the limit of the western Allied advance. Some British and American commanders protested. Stopping at the Elbe would mean that the Soviets would have the honor of taking Berlin, and though they were military allies, on a political level the communist Soviet Union and the capitalist west were having increasing difficulty resolving their differences. And many were already predicting that the end of the war would bring new levels of tension between these nations. But Eisenhower was more concerned with the present situation, and also knew going farther than the Elbe might again stretch his supply lines.

With the Nazi capital now theirs, the Soviets entered Berlin on April 16. Over the next two weeks, the most violent, horrific, and devastating battle since Stalingrad raged as 2.5 million Soviet troops painstakingly eliminated the last remnants of the German army. In an underground bunker underneath the Reich Chancellery, Hitler continued to encourage his troops to fight to the death. Though some of his commanders urged him to escape to his retreat in the Bavarian Alps where he and his few followers could organize a guerilla resistance, Hitler refused. He would stay in Berlin until the end.

The end was coming fast. On April, 21st, the last resistance in the Ruhr pocket surrendered, and four days later, American and Soviet troops linked up at Torgau on the Elbe River, cutting Germany in half.

As April drew to a close, the Soviets were just a block away from the Chancellery. On April 30, after marrying his longtime fiancée, Eva Braun, and writing his last will and testament, Adolf Hitler committed suicide.

With the Fuhrer's death went the one thing preventing the German army from surrendering. On May 2, the Berlin Garrison surrendered, and the only real fighting remained along the eastern front, where German troops desperately fought their way west, preferring to surrender to the western Allies, who treated their prisoners far better than the Soviets. In the early hours of May, 7 1945, in a small schoolhouse in Reims, France, what remained of the German government signed an unconditional surrender treaty to the Allies.

May 8, 1945 at 11:01 pm, the war in Europe was over.

Notes and References

The content of this book is my personal, original telling of the events and circumstances of World War II. While there is no intent to copy or quote a source without acknowledging the source, I do not believe any of the content herein is a duplicate of any original work by another author.

In addition to conducting 50+ interviews with veterans of all conflicts, I have read dozens of books on the topic of World War II. Here is a partial list of those materials for your reference.

Ambrose, Stephen. *The Good Fight: How World War II Was Won*. New York: Simon & Schuster, 2003

Bott, Lawrence. *Memories of an Infantry Combat Medic in World War 2*. Columbus: Self Published, 2005

Brinkley, Douglas. *World War II The Allied Counteroffensive: The Documents, Speeches, Diaries, and Newspaper Reporting that Defined World War II* . New York: Henry Holt and Company, 2003

Brokaw, Tom. *The Greatest Generation*. New York: Random House Inc, 2004
Cawthorne, Nigel. Tyrants: History's 100 Most Evil Despots and Dictators. New York: Metro Books, 2012

Darman, Peter. *World War II: Fact and Quiz Book*. New York:Brown Reference Group, 2010

Dowswell, Paul, *War Stories*. London: Usbourne Publishing Ltd, 2006.

Frank, Anne. *The Diary of a Young Girl: The Definitive Edition*. New York: Anchor Books, A division of Random House, 1991.

Garner, Joe and Cronkite, Walter, and Kurtis, Bill. *We Interrupt This Broadcast: Updated Second Edition: The Events that Stopped Our Lives... from the Hindenburg Explosion to the Death of John F. Kennedy Jr*. Naperville: Sourcebooks, 2000.

Gragg, Rod. *Letters Home From World War II: from Foxholes and Flight Decks*. New York: Fall River Press, 2009

Hildebrandt, Alexandra. *The Wall: Figures. Facts*. Berlin: Verl. Haus am Checkpoint Charlie, 2008

Mann, Chris, Dr. *Great Battles of World War II: Military Encounters that Defined the Future*. Bath, UK: Parragon Books Ltd, 2009
Mann, Chris, Dr. *Great Battles of World War II*. Bath, UK: Parragon Books Ltd, 2008

Rooney, Andy. *My War*. New York: PublicAffairs, 1995

Shaara, Jeff. *The Steel Wave*. New York: Random House Inc, 2008

Sheri Bell-Rehwoldt. *Great World War II Projects*. Chicago: Nomad Press, 2006

Showalter, Dennis. *Hitler's Panzers*. New York: Penguin Group Inc,2009

Taylor, Theodore. *Battle in the Arctic Seas*. New York/ London: Sterling, 1976

The Editors of the Army Times. *The Banners and the Glory: The Story of General Douglas MacAurthur*. New York: G.P. Putnam's Sons, 1965

Vat, Dan van der. *The Pacific Campaign* . New York: Simon & Schuster, 2006
Wales, Ken & Pooling, David. Sea of Glory. Nashville: Broadman & Holdman, 2001

West, Rodney MD. *Honolulu Prepares for Japan's Attack: May 15, 1940 to December 8, 1941*. Honolulu: Jane Estioko and Ray Sandla, 2008

White, David and Murphy, Daniel P, PHD. *The Everything World War Two Book 2nd Edition*. Avon: Adams Media, an F+W Publications Company, 2007

Voices from the Front

Voices from the Front is a non-profit organization founded to preserve the stories of our nation's veterans. Started as an Eagle Project in January 2012, the organization has interviewed nearly 200 veterans from all conflicts. The archive even includes one firsthand account from World War I!

Voices from the Front is still actively seeking volunteers to help achieve our goal of collecting 1,000 stories. You can help!

Veterans - If you are a veteran and would like to share your story, please contact us.

Volunteer - if you know a veteran who would like to share his or her story, if you would like to interview veterans, write and edit veteran stories, help in audio or video editing, or work on the website, please contact us.

Donations – if you are interested in making a donation to our cause, please contact us.

You can find out more about Voices from the Front and read firsthand accounts of veterans at our website, www.voicesfromthefront.org.